Few people have had greater in ☐☐☐☐ than the fifth-century bishop Cy ☐☐☐☐ circles, his reputation has taken a ☐☐☐☐ ....ore, and Cyril's life and teaching have ᴜᴇᴇɴ significantly misunderstood. Daniel Hames' little book sets the record straight and gives us a striking window into the importance—and the brilliance—of one of the Christian Church's greatest thinkers. You'll come away from this book not only with a new appreciation for the Cyril you never knew, but far more important, with a deepened sense of wonder at the depths of the Gospel.

Donald Fairbairn

Professor of Early Christianity, Gordon-Conwell Theological
Seminary, and Professor of Historical and Systematic Theology,
Union School of Theology, Hamilton, Massachusetts

To be a Christian is to believe that the man Jesus Christ is none other than God the Son come down from heaven to save humanity. While this claim might seem obvious to those of us who know, love, and follow Jesus, you might not realize that we owe an enormous debt of gratitude to a fifth-century bishop and lover of Christ known as Cyril of Alexandria for articulating, defending, and preserving this biblical truth in this way. Sadly, for many of us who have grown up in evangelical and reformed churches, church fathers like Cyril have long been neglected as a resource for study and devotion. Thankfully, Daniel Hames has written a book that goes a long way toward helping us recover Cyril's teaching for the church today. Drawing from an impressive grasp of Cyril's life and writings, Dr. Hames surveys his biography, summarizes his theology, and considers his legacy in a study that is as enjoyable as it is informative. Reading this book will grow your appreciation for Cyril and, even more, your love for Jesus Christ, the divine Son incarnate. I highly recommend it.

John W Tweeddale

Vice-President and Professor of Theology,
Reformation Bible College, Sanford, Florida

EARLY CHURCH FATHERS
SERIES EDITORS
MICHAEL A. G. HAYKIN & SHAWN J. WILHITE

CYRIL
OF HIS LIFE
& IMPACT
ALEXAN-
DRIA

DANIEL HAMES

CHRISTIAN
FOCUS

Scripture quotations are from *The Holy Bible, English Standard Version*, copyright © 2001 by Crossway Bibles, a division of Good News Publishers. Used by permission. All rights reserved. ESV Text Edition: 2007.

Copyright © Daniel Hames 2024

paperback ISBN 978-1-5271-1133-2
ebook ISBN 978-1-5271-1211-7

10 9 8 7 6 5 4 3 2 1

Published in 2024
by
Christian Focus Publications Ltd,
Geanies House, Fearn, Ross-shire,
IV20 1TW, Great Britain.

www.christianfocus.com

Cover design by
MOOSE77

Printed and bound by
Bell & Bain, Glasgow

CONTENTS

DEDICATION

For my Sarah

SERIES PREFACE

On Reading the Church Fathers

By common definition, the Church Fathers are those early Christian authors who wrote between the close of the first century, right after the death of the last of the apostles, namely the apostle John, and the middle of the eighth century. In other words, those figures who were active in the life of the Church between Ignatius of Antioch and Clement of Rome, who penned writings at the very beginning of the second century, and the Venerable Bede and John of Damascus, who stood at the close of antiquity and the onset of the Middle Ages. Far too many evangelicals in the modern day know next to nothing about these figures. I will never forget being asked to give a mini-history conference at a church in southern Ontario. I suggested three talks on three figures from Latin-speaking North Africa: Perpetua, Cyprian, and Augustine. The leadership of the church came back to me seeking a different set of names, since they had never heard of the first two figures, and while they had heard of the third name, the famous bishop of Hippo Regius, they really knew nothing about him. I gave them another list of post-Reformation figures for the mini-conference, but privately thought that not knowing anything about these figures was possibly a very good reason to have a conference on them! I suspect that such ignorance is quite widespread among those who call themselves Evangelicals – hence the importance of this small series of studies on a select number of Church Fathers, to educate and inform God's people about their forebears in the faith.

Past Appreciation for the Fathers

How different is the modern situation from the past, when many of our Evangelical and Reformed forebears knew and treasured the writings of the ancient church. The French Reformer John Calvin, for example, was ever a keen student of the Church Fathers. He did not always agree with them, even when it came to one of his favourite authors, namely, Augustine. But he was deeply aware of the value of knowing their thought and drawing upon the riches of their written works for elucidating the Christian faith in his own day. And in the seventeenth century, the Puritan theologian John Owen, rightly called the 'Calvin of England' by some of his contemporaries, was not slow to turn to the experience of the one he called 'holy Austin,' namely Augustine, to provide him with a pattern of God the Holy Spirit's work in conversion.

Yet again, when the Particular Baptist John Gill was faced with the anti-Trinitarianism of the Deist movement in the early eighteenth century, and other Protestant bodies – for instance, the English Presbyterians, the General Baptists, and large tracts of Anglicanism – were unable to retain a firm grasp on this utterly vital biblical doctrine, Gill turned to the Fathers to help him elucidate the biblical teaching regarding the blessed Trinity. Gill's example in this regard influenced other Baptists such as John Sutcliff, pastor of the Baptist cause in Olney, where John Newton also ministered. Sutcliff was so impressed by the *Letter* to *Diognetus*, which he wrongly supposed to have been written by Justin Martyr, that he translated it for *The Biblical Magazine*, a Calvinistic publication with a small circulation. He sent it to the editor of this periodical with the commendation that this second-century work is 'one of the most valuable pieces of ecclesiastical antiquity.'

One Final Caveat

One final word about the Fathers recommended in this small series of essays. The Fathers are not Scripture. They are senior conversation partners about Scripture and its meaning. We listen to them respectfully, but are not afraid to disagree when they err. As the Reformers rightly argued, the writings of the Fathers must be subject to Scripture. John Jewel, the Anglican apologist, put it well when he stated in 1562:

> But what say we of the fathers, Augustine, Ambrose, Jerome, Cyprian, etc.? What shall we think of them, or what account may we make of them? They be interpreters of the word of God. They were learned men, and learned fathers; the instruments of the mercy of God, and vessels full of grace. We despise them not, we read them, we reverence them, and give thanks unto God for them. They were witnesses unto the truth, they were worthy pillars and ornaments in the church of God. Yet may they not be compared with the word of God. We may not build upon them: we may not make them the foundation and warrant of our conscience: we may not put our trust in them. Our trust is in the name of the Lord.

Michael A. G. Haykin
The Southern Baptist Theological Seminary
Louisville, Kentucky, U.S.A.

FOREWORD

Reputations rise and fall, but when it comes to Cyril of Alexandria, the steep difference between his vast historical importance and his current obscurity is simply shocking. What other major theologian has managed this kind of vanishing act over the centuries? He contributed so much to the history of doctrine that he was once well enshrined as a standard Christological reference point for the later ecumenical councils, for medieval theologians, and for the early Protestants. But today, even among well-educated readers who can pride themselves on a decent amount of Patristic knowledge, Cyril of Alexandria seems like some sort of obscure figure only to be encountered in advanced courses of study. His name doesn't strike us as fitting among the big names like Irenaeus, Athanasius, Gregory of Nyssa, or Augustine; he seems more at home with middling figures like Eustathius, Epiphanius, and Hilary of Poitiers; maybe even down among the certifiably minor figures like Amphilochius of Iconium or Phoebadius of Agen. Who? Exactly.

Just how important Cyril has been since his death in 444, and just how valuable he remains for Christian theology today, is what Daniel Hames undertakes to explain in this fine book. Hames also explores some of the factors that have contributed to modern neglect of Cyril, how English-speaking Christians lost touch with Cyril somewhere in the Victorian era, and how current scholarship is finally giving him the attention he deserves (including translations of major works). Hames draws on all the right resources to commend Cyril to a wide audience of contemporary readers: he narrates the history, explains the controversies, introduces the personalities, and connects the theological dots.

It is this theological dot-connecting, above all, that makes Cyril worth retrieving. Hames rightly presents Cyril of Alexandria as possessing the kind of theological mind that conveys Christian doctrine not as a disconnected set of doctrinal items on a list, but as a joined-up and organically living system of spiritual understanding. Cyril never got lost in the details. Even when he had to descend all the way into the finest points of theological argument, or when the stridency of controversy required careful parsing and jealous guarding of key terms, Cyril always kept his focus on the main thing. That main thing is not a thing but a person, Jesus Christ. Cyril's characteristically unitive understanding of the one person in two natures is the great, central through-line that holds together his own theological synthesis just as it holds together the conciliar Christology of the ancient church.

In Hames' deft account of Cyril's theology, contemporary readers can see how the great truths of the ancient church's Christology support and nourish the evangelical experience of salvation. Cyril's unitive Christology enables us to tell the story of the Son's eternal communion with the Father, his assumption of human nature, his incarnate accomplishment of redemption, and his victorious completion of the purposes of salvation, as the unified story it is, centered on that singular, selfsame savior. His focus on the person of Christ yields a deeper understanding of the personal nature of salvation, which turns out to be much more than a mere rearrangement of human possibilities, or some sort of action-at-a-distance that delivers specified benefits. Salvation, when consistently joined up with Trinity and incarnation in Cyrilline fashion, shows itself to be something higher and more relationally intimate. A deep respect for the word of God in Scripture, an exalted doctrine of God, a unitive Christology, and a very high doctrine of salvation, all come together in the vast spiritual vision of Cyril of Alexandria, as in almost no other ancient Christian theologian.

Having said so much, it is tempting to backpedal a bit and admit that this great synthesis of Christology and soteriology is not somehow the unique property of Cyril. It can be found, after all, in numerous great teachers from early Christianity's classical period, and nearly all of it is drawn from Scripture, often word for word. Christian theology could, in fact, put together and proclaim this entire well-integrated package of Christ and salvation without necessarily taking recourse to this one teacher from fifth-century Alexandria, or naming the name of Cyril. This is true. And in the dark days of our recent neglect of Cyril, we often enough succeeded in conveying his main ideas more or less anonymously. But for most of the history of the faith, theologians have been well aware of how much they owed Cyril for his contribution to honing our ability to proclaim the main thing with clarity, coherence, and power. Daniel Hames' timely and spirited introduction to Cyril's life and impact summons us to rejoin that company.

Fred Sanders
Torrey Honors College, Biola University

A CHRONOLOGY OF CYRIL

c376	Cyril is born in Theodosios, Egypt
394	Cyril goes to the Desert of Nitria for monastic education
399	Cyril leaves the desert
403	Cyril attends the Synod of the Oak in Constantinople
428	The beginning of the Nestorian controversy
431	Cyril presides at the Council of Ephesus

INTRODUCTION

While I was at university, I remember telling a friend, 'I'm definitely a Christian, and I definitely believe in God. But I don't know where Jesus fits in it all anymore.' Although I was probably being a little dramatic, I was sincerely asking questions about the evangelical faith in which I'd been raised. Who is God? What is He like and how do we come to know Him? What does it mean for a person when they become a Christian?

We may be tempted to think that these questions belong in a children's Sunday School class or in the first few weeks of an evangelistic course. They are the basics: the ABCs of the faith. Dare we say it, they're the *simple* questions. Many of us – especially those who like to read and talk theology – would tend to leave these behind and wade into the 'deeper waters' of other doctrines or practices. Controversy, curiosity, and complexity beckon!

Strange, then, that these foundational questions should occupy the life and work of one of the early church's most influential and important figures. Cyril of Alexandria, a fifth century bishop with global influence and significant theological ability, devoted his ministry not to ivory tower navel-gazing, nor to academic showboating, but to the basics. Through just the sort of controversy, curiosity, and complexity that some hanker after, Cyril's focus was undivided on these fundamentals. The reason was that he could see that some of the Church's best-known preachers and writers were giving the wrong answers to these questions. Cyril would see a looming danger when popular pastors, clever writers, and smart political operators drew everyday Christians away from scriptural clarity on the identity and nature of God and the salvation He has given. For Cyril, nothing was more important than safeguarding the truth that had been passed down from ancient times.

The Only Answer

There is a well-known joke about the children's Sunday School teacher who asks her class: 'What is grey, has a bushy tail, eats nuts, and lives in trees?' The story goes that one child responds, 'I know the answer is meant to be "Jesus", but it sounds like a squirrel to me.' Even little children can become over-familiar with the routine and perhaps roll their eyes when the answer, once again, is 'Jesus'. Some readers will have sung almost to death the line, 'It's all about you, Jesus'. But Cyril would assure us that it is neither twee nor glib to affirm that these familiar instincts are theologically spot on.

The controversy that came to be the headline over Cyril's life centred on the identity of Jesus Christ. Cyril's contemporary in Constantinople, Nestorius, spoke about the Lord in a way that virtually nobody else in the Church at the time could recognise in Scripture or the Christian tradition. He saw Jesus as a man like us but 'assumed' by, and given a special relationship *with*, the eternal Son. Although Christ *appeared as one person*, there were *two* behind the scenes: Mary's son and God the Son. Cyril's response to Nestorius was to defend the truth that the Church had always taught. The man Jesus was none other than God the Son Himself, personally stepping into our humanity to save us and bring us into fellowship with His Father. When Cyril came up against Nestorius, he could see that what a person thinks of Jesus Christ truly changes *everything*. If God and humanity do not really come together in this one person, then God and humanity cannot come together in *salvation* either. If God has not come into the world in the incarnation, then God has never really been near to us. In other words, Cyril saw that Jesus truly is the answer to all our questions about God, salvation, and everything – and that to have the wrong Jesus is to risk all. As Paul wrote to the Corinthians, 'another Jesus' means 'a different gospel' (2 Cor. 11:4).

Cyril's tenacious Christ-centeredness shaped the faith of the Church, especially at the Council of Ephesus (431) and the landmark Council of Chalcedon (451). His theological efforts have made their mark on us whenever we speak of Christ's 'two natures' or the 'hypostatic union'; or perhaps more commonly when we sing, 'Forbid it, Lord, that I should boast / save in *the death of Christ my God*' and 'Amazing love! how can it be / that *thou, my God, should die for me?*' Cyril stood for truth of 'one Lord Jesus Christ', a single person who is true God and true man. The same one who was with the Father in the beginning before all ages has taken humanity, suffered and died, and risen to life – all *for us*, and *for our salvation*. Cyril's heart was that believers would consciously and joyfully place Jesus Christ front and centre in their understanding of God and their salvation. He was, before anything else, a pastor taking care of a flock who needed to know assurance, grow in intimacy with God, and worship Him in spirit and truth. For all this, he knew, they needed to see and enjoy the *real* Jesus.

Meeting Cyril

I first met Cyril in 2009 as I began postgraduate theological study in Oxford and have been fascinated with him ever since. I have my friend Michael Reeves to thank for making the introduction and for showing me the significance of Cyril's theology. Since then, Donald Fairbairn and John Behr have been especially generous in giving me their time, as well as writing some of the best material available on Cyril and his theology. With their help, and with books by John McGuckin, Thomas Weinandy and Daniel Keating, Norman Russell, and others, I set out on master's research in Oxford under Mark Edwards and, later, a PhD at the VU Amsterdam with Cornelis van der Kooi, Matthias Smalbrugge, and Katya Tolstoj – both with Cyril's thought as a central focus.

When approaching Cyril for the first time, people tend to bump into certain roadblocks that have accumulated over time, and often cause them to set out with a fairly negative picture of the man. These are not always easy to shift. People hear that he is an 'Alexandrian' and so prone to fits of ridiculous allegorical interpretation of Scripture (unlike the sensible and literal 'Antiochenes'). We read in popular textbooks that he was a nasty and manipulative bully, demolishing churches, bribing officials, and commanding vast armies of militant monks. It is sometimes said that Nestorius was no Nestorian and wasn't saying anything nearly as dangerous as Cyril claimed, and that Cyril simply wanted a fight. And there is the rumour that Cyril murdered the philosopher Hypatia. With the wisdom of the real experts named above, I have tried to address and challenge all these things in this book. I hope my efforts will help people still getting to know Cyril to have a much clearer picture of him and of his theology. With some of these misunderstandings (and some outright lies) cleared up, Cyril is a theologian well worth spending time with. Some of his writings are still not available in English, but many are – and in good, contemporary translations too. His little book, *On the Unity of Christ*, translated by John McGuckin for SVS Press (1995) is a good place to begin. His *Commentary on John* translated by David Maxwell in IVP's Ancient Christian Texts series (2013, 2015) is a weightier, two-volume read. Cyril's two most important letters to Nestorius can be read easily for free online, including at www.unionpublishing. org. As far as secondary literature goes, John McGuckin's *Saint Cyril of Alexandria and the Christological Controversy* is a superb in-depth study, and Donald Fairbairn's *Grace and Christology in the Early Church* is the must-read analysis of Cyril's theology.

As well as the people named above, I want to thank Ben Lloyd who acted as my research assistant one summer as I wrote, Timothy Ezat, and a handful of students at Union School of Theology, whose dissertations on Cyril have sharpened my understanding over the years: Sam Cotten, Pete Gower, Chris Murphy, and Ben Welchman. I am thankful, too, for the wise and kind editorial guidance of Michael Haykin and Shawn Wilhite.

About this Book

This book begins with some history and biography of Cyril and then a brief chapter setting up the dynamics of the controversy with Nestorius. The chapters on Jesus, God, and salvation are a look into Cyril's theology, especially in the light of the theological battles he was fighting. The final chapter and afterword survey his influence on the church immediately after his lifetime and highlight some of the ways we might turn to Cyril today as we navigate the questions and debates of our own time. I hope you will enjoy meeting Cyril as you read this book. He is controversial, daring, amusing, and a brilliant reader of Scripture. More, though, I hope you will be delighted afresh at the glory and goodness of Jesus Christ. Cyril has helped me answer my naïve question at university about where Jesus fits more than most.

Jesus is the image of the invisible God, the firstborn of all creation, the creator and sustainer of all things. He is the head of the church, the firstborn from the dead, and in Him – in His human flesh and blood – the fullness of God was pleased to dwell, right from the moment He was conceived by the Holy

Spirit in the Virgin Mary. And when our incarnate Lord and God suffered and died on the cross, He not only cleansed us from sin, but brought us peace and reconciliation with God (Col 1:15-20). Jesus *really* is the Alpha and Omega: the first and last word on knowing God, on living the Christian life, on our future eternal hope. He is God *with* us and God *for* us. What better or truer answer could we give to the most important questions that define and disturb us?

Daniel Hames
Oxford
Feast of Cyril of Alexandria, 27 June 2023

1

THE MAN FROM ALEXANDRIA

Alexandria began its life as Rhacotis, a sleepy port town, standing proud on a limestone ridge amid the marshes where the Mediterranean meets the freshwater Lake Mareotis.[1] Alexander the Great had arrived (c. 331 BC) and founded a city there – named, of course, after himself – as a Greek outpost in Egypt, with the hope it would become a centre for commerce.[2] Although Alexander immediately left Egypt, never to return, his dreams for the place certainly came true.

The city grew into a heaving metropolis and a hotspot for international trade. For almost three centuries after Alexander, the Ptolemies ruled over their empire from the city, quickly swelling its population with eager migrants.[3] The famous lighthouse was finished in 247 BC and, standing over 100 metres high on the island of Pharos at the mouth of the harbour, cast the light of a giant furnace over the ocean at night and

1. Strabo, *The Geography of Strabo: Book 17*, vol. VIII, trans. Horace Leonard Jones (Cambridge, MA: Harvard University Press, 1932), 31 (17.1.8).

2. Arrian, *The Anabasis of Alexander*, trans. E. J. Chinnock (London: Hodder and Stoughton, 1884), 140ff (Book III, Chapter I).

3. Strabo, *Geography*, 17.1.8.

mirrored the sun's light by day.[4] Set along the shoreline in the Royal Quarter, was the Museum, a huge complex not unlike a university campus, dedicated to illumination of the academic kind. Here, literary scholars and scientific researchers exchanged the latest ideas while milling around ornamental colonnades and extensive gardens. Their food and lodgings were provided by the administrator, a priest of Serapis, the Alexandrians' favourite sun god.[5] At the heart of the Museum was the Great Library, a collection reputed to contain hundreds of thousands of scrolls, ranging from the works of Aristotle to a portion of the Septuagint (the Greek translation of the Old Testament, originally compiled in the city).[6] Alexandria's reputation for learning was celebrated. It could count among its famous sons Euclid, considered the father of geometry and active there around 300 BC;[7] a chief librarian, Eratosthenes (c. 276-195 BC), who was the first to calculate the circumference of the earth and the tilt of its axis,[8] and the renowned Jewish philosopher, Philo (c. 20 BC–AD 50), who was born and lived in the city.[9]

4.   Pliny the Elder, *Natural History*, 36.18; Strabo, *Geography*, 17.6. See also, L. Sprague de Camp, 'The "Darkhouse" of Alexandria' in *Technology and Culture* 6, no. 3 [1965], 423-427).

5.   Strabo, *Geography*, 17.1.8. See also Mostafa El-Abbadi, *The Life and Fate of the Ancient Library of Alexandria* (Paris: UNESCO/UNDP, 1990) and P. M. Fraser, *Ptolomaic Alexandria*, 3 volumes (Oxford: Clarendon Press, 1972). The Museum is sometimes known as the Mouseiun.

6.   Aristeas, *The Letter of Aristeas*, trans. H. St. J. Thackeray (London: SPCK, 1918); Roger S. Bagnall, 'Alexandria: Library of Dreams' in *Proceedings of the American Philosophical Society*, vol. 146, no. 4 (2002), 348-62; William W. Fortenbaugh and Eckart Schütrumpf (eds.), *Demetrius of Phalerum: Text, Translation, and Discussion* (New York: Routledge, 2017), 331-45. The exact connection between the Museum and the Library is not totally clear.

7.   William Trollope, *First Book of Euclid's Elements* (London: William Foster, 1847).

8.   Duane W. Roller, *Eratosthenes' Geography* (Princeton: Princeton University Press, 2010).

9.   Jean Daniélou, *Philo of Alexandria*, trans. James G. Colbert (Cambridge: James Clarke & Co, 2014).

Cyril's Alexandria

By the fifth century AD, Alexandria was a distinctly Christian place. Tradition has it that Mark, the disciple of Jesus and writer of the second Gospel, had visited the city twice. The first trip was a successful missionary endeavour, winning converts and even ordaining a bishop to oversee the new church there. The second was to end in his martyrdom. Presiding at Holy Communion on Easter Day in AD 68, he was captured by enraged pagan citizens. He had been worshipping Christ on what happened to be the feast day of Serapis, so a rope was tied around his neck, and he was dragged through the streets until he was dead.[10] Yet, Alexandria had seen the slowly growing influence of Christianity on its culture and politics. The conversion of the Roman Emperor Constantine in AD 312 meant that Alexandria, like other major cities in the empire, soon filled with converts, more than a dozen churches, and even Christian businesses.[11] Although the Library and Museum had long since been left to deteriorate by this time, the Alexandrian tradition of scholarship was still alive and well.[12] There was an influential theological college (possibly founded at Mark's first visit) which taught Christian doctrine for nearly 400 years, stretching to the time of Didymus the Blind in 398.[13]

---

10. See B. Evetts, *Patrologia Orientalis* 1 (Paris: Librairie de Paris, 1907), 142–148.

11. Christopher Haas, *Alexandria in Late Antiquity: Topography and Social Conflict* (London: John Hopkins University Press, 2006), 173–206; Norman Russell, Theophilus of Alexandria (London: Routledge, 2006), 4–5.

12. It is worth noting that the Library (which may, in fact, have been multiple libraries) was never destroyed in one cataclysmic event, as is sometimes imagined. Over decades, it was damaged at various times, including during Julius Caesar's siege in 48BC, and by fires. But its downfall was almost certainly due more to declining membership and underfunding than disaster. The last recorded members of the Museum are in the AD 260s, and it likely ceased its business in the 270s. See Bagnall, *Library of Dreams*, 356–60, and El-Abbadi, *The Life and Fate of the Ancient Library of Alexandria*, 167–72. See also, Roy Macleod (ed.) *The Library of Alexandria: Centre of Learning in the Ancient World* (London: I. B. Tauris, 2004), Jean-Arcady Meyer, *The Rise and Fall of the Library of Alexandria* (Cambridge: Cambridge Scholars Publishing, 2023).

13. See W. H. Oliver, 'The Heads of the Catechetical School in Alexandria', *Verbum et Ecclesia* 36, no. 1 (2015), and 'The catechetical school in Alexandria', *Verbum et*

Alexandria's bishops or 'popes' oversaw not only the churches and congregations of that city, but also acted as the lynchpin and archbishop ('patriarch') of all the other bishops of Egypt. This meant that they appointed the other local bishops and supervised their ministries. These men also wielded increasingly significant civic and political firepower as years went by.[14] What was once a deeply pagan city they now called 'the most glorious and Christ-loving city of the Alexandrians.'[15]

The Christian population was apparently the majority by Cyril's time, but the city was nevertheless a diverse, bustling melting-pot.[16] Prosperous and productive, it was known for its manufacture of papyrus, luxury goods (whether blown glass or confectionary), and medicines from doctors as famous as Egyptian linen.[17] Lively trades like these, along with its impressive academic heritage, meant the continual convergence of people from all over the world. The population had to absorb cultural and religious differences as Jewish, pagan, and Christian communities lived side-by-side. This was rarely a peaceful co-existence and the tensions played out in very public ways. Alexandrians of all backgrounds loved to gather at the theatre, for live music, in bath houses, and in taverns. They were especially fond of large-scale sporting spectacles like the horseracing in the hippodrome. Two teams clashed at these events, the Blues (*Venetoi*) and the Greens (*Prasinoi*), and the population divided themselves between them. Allegiance to the Blues or the Greens seemed to mean something more than sports fandom, but also embraced political and social identity. As large and diverse crowds gathered for these events, the city

Ecclesia 36, no. 1 (2015); Norman Russell, *Cyril of Alexandria* (London: Routledge, 2000), 10.

14. See Norman Russell, *Theophilus of Alexandria*, 3–44.

15. Haas, *Alexandria in Late Antiquity*, 14.

16. Norman Russell, *Theophilus of Alexandria* (London: Routledge, 2006), 4–5.

17. Haas, *Alexandria in Late Antiquity*, 33–36.

authorities took the opportunity to communicate messages and to carry out the public punishment of criminals.[18] In such a febrile atmosphere, it was very common for street fighting and looting to break out. Socrates Scholasticus (380–439) wrote that,

> The Alexandrians are more delighted with tumult than any other people: and if they can find a pretext, they will break forth into the most intolerable excesses; nor is it scarcely possible to check their impetuosity until there has been much bloodshed.[19]

The description is perhaps a touch over-dramatic, but there is no question that Alexandria had a well-deserved reputation for rioting.[20]

Heat and Light

Alexandria was a cauldron of both heat and light. Political power blended with social unease; great learning mingled with violence and strife. It is not surprising that, from such an explosive environment, a figure like Cyril would emerge. A man of substantial intellect and force of will, a fighter of heresy and unafraid of controversy – yet a local pastor, biblical scholar, and lover of Christ all the same. He has been described as a 'Marmite' figure, dividing opinion: 'people either love him or hate him'.[21] It is true. On the one hand, in the seventh century,

---

18. Haas, *Alexandria in Late Antiquity*, 63–69.

19. Socrates, *Ecclesiastical History*, 7.13, Philip Schaff and Henry Wace (eds.) *Socrates, Sozomenus: Church Histories* (trans. A. C. Zenos) vol. 2, A Select Library of the Nicene and Post-Nicene Fathers of the Christian Church, Second Series (New York: Christian Literature Company, 1890), 159.

20. Haas, *Alexandria in Late Antiquity*, 10–14. See also, Lauren Kaplow, 'Religious and Intercommunal Violence in Alexandria in the 4th and 5th centuries CE' in *Hirundo: The McGill Journal of Classical Studies* vol. IV, 2–26 (2006) and Edward J. Watts, *Riot in Alexandria: Tradition and Group Dynamics in Late Antique Pagan and Christian Communities* (Berkeley: University of California Press, 2010).

21. Anthony N. S. Lane, 'Review of *The Theology of St Cyril of Alexandria: A Critical Appreciation* by Thomas G. Weinandy and Daniel A. Keating,' *Journal of Theological Studies*, 56, no. 2 (2005): 695.

Anastasius of Sinai called him 'the seal of the fathers'[22] and, in 1883, Pope Leo XIII named Cyril the twentieth 'Doctor of the Church'. He shares a feast day in the Eastern Church with the great Athanasius and is held in high regard by many. Yet, on the other hand, he has a lingering reputation as a bully, a fiendishly corrupt political operator, and a theological fanatic. On hearing the news of Cyril's death in 444, one theological opponent is supposed to have written:

> At last and with difficulty the villain has gone. The good and gentle pass away all too soon; the bad prolong their life for years... [T]he Lord has lopped him off like a plague and 'taken away the reproach from Israel.' His survivors are indeed delighted at his departure. The dead, maybe, are sorry. There is some ground of alarm lest they should be so much annoyed at his company as to send him back to us... Great care must then be taken, and it is especially your holiness's business to undertake this duty, to tell the guild of undertakers to lay a very big and heavy stone upon his grave, for fear he should come back again... He will be stoned not only by ghosts learned in divine law, but also by Nimrod, Pharaoh and Sennacherib, or any other of God's enemies.[23]

Cyril was very much *of Alexandria*: learned, powerful, and tumultuous. But there is no escaping his significant influence on the theology of the early church and the generations that followed. While many historians and theologians have written him off, falling into easy caricatures and believing every aspersion

22. Anastasius of Sinai, hod. (=viae dux) 7.101 in K. H. Uthemann, Corpus Christianorum Series Graeca 8 (Turnhout: Brepols, 1981), 107 cited in Stephen J. Davis, *Coptic Christology in Practice: Incarnation and Divine Participation in Late and Medieval Egypt* (Oxford: OUP, 2008), 28.

23. Theodoret of Cyrus, "Letters of the Blessed Theodoret, Bishop of Cyrus," in *Theodoret, Jerome, Gennadius, Rufinus: Historical Writings, Etc.*, ed. Philip Schaff and Henry Wace, trans. Blomfield Jackson, vol. 3, A Select Library of the Nicene and Post-Nicene Fathers of the Christian Church, Second Series (New York: Christian Literature Company, 1892), 346.

cast upon him, there is far more to the man than controversy.[24] Like Alexandria and its beacon on Pharos, the heat comes with light. Cyril's keen theological thought and biblical insight are no less a providential gift to the church today than they were in his own time.

Cyril's Early Years

Cyril was born around AD 376 (or 378) in the small town of Theodosius (or Didouseya). He was raised 85 miles west of Alexandria in what became a prominent Christian household. His mother and her brother, Theophilus, had moved to Alexandria as orphans, but were both baptised by the great Athanasius, who later became Theophilus' personal mentor and eventually his employer. Cyril was still a boy of seven when his uncle became Patriarch of Alexandria in 385.[25]

He recalls learning the Scriptures under Theophilus' instruction and, as the young man grew up, it appears that his uncle encouraged him toward the priesthood, sending him along to the Catechetical School.[26] It is possible that Cyril came directly under the guidance of Didymus the Blind, the last head of the school, taking classes in theology twice a week, alongside a rhythm of daily prayers and Holy Communion.[27] When Cyril reached about 20 years old, Theophilus packed his nephew off to the Nitrian Desert to continue his education and formation in the famous monastic community there. For five years, Cyril lived an ascetic life in a community of a few thousand monks, likely

---

24. See chapter six for a brief look at Cyril's reception over the centuries.

25. It is worth noting that Athanasius died in 373 before Cyril was born, so the two never met.

26. Cyril recalled this during the Council of Ephesus, 'We studied the holy Scriptures from a tender age and were reared in the arms of orthodox and holy fathers.' Richard Price, trans., *The Council of Ephesus of 431: Documents and Proceedings*, TTH 72 (Liverpool: Liverpool University Press, 2020), 394.

27. Pierre Évieux, *Cyrille d'Alexandrie: Lettres Festales, I–VI*, Sources chrétiennes 372 (Paris: Les Editions du Cerf, 1991), 13.

under the mentorship of Serapion the Wise.[28] It was rumoured that he had a near-photographic memory for learning Scripture, which he read in vast quantities.

> He used to stand before his teacher studying, with a sword of iron in his hand; and if he felt an inclination to sleep, he pricked him with the sword, and so he woke up again; and during most of his nights he would read through in a single night the Four Gospels, and the Catholic Epistles, and the Acts, and the first Epistle of the Blessed Paul, namely, that addressed to the Romans; and on the morrow after this, Cyril's teacher would know, by looking at his face, that he had studied all night. And the grace of God was with Cyril, so that when he had read a book once, he knew it by heart; and in these years in the desert, he learnt by heart all the canonical books.[29]

As well as biblical studies, he was plunged into doctrine and history, shaped by the influence of Anthony of Egypt, Basil of Caesarea, and Athanasius.[30] Theophilus eventually recalled Cyril to Alexandria where it seems he became his uncle's assistant and was ordained a reader in the church, marking the beginning of a ministry of preaching and teaching.[31]

We do not know a great deal about the next few years of Cyril's life back in the big city. John O'Keefe writes that Cyril's later 'remarkably human' letters reveal a keen sailor (or, at least, passenger), a lover of good food, and a man who may have sometimes battled to control his temper.[32] His works, full of references to an array of literature from both the Christian and pagan traditions, reveal a man who read widely and loved

28. Lois Farag, *St Cyril of Alexandria: A New Testament Exegete* (Piscataway, NJ: Gorgias Press, 2014), 16-21.

29. Severus of El Ashmunein, *History of the Coptic Patriarchs*, 11 (Patrologia Orientalis 1:429).

30. Severus, *History of the Coptic Patriarchs*, 11 (*Patrologia Orientalis* 1:429).

31. Évieux, *Lettres Festales*, I–VI, 21.

32. John J. O'Keefe, *St Cyril of Alexandria. Festal Letters* 1-12 (Washington DC: Catholic University of America Press, 2009), 7.

the scholarly work of following leads in his study like any good researcher.[33] We do know that, in 403, Cyril attended the Synod of the Oak in Constantinople with Theophilus, the council in which John Chrysostom was deposed as Archbishop of Constantinople. The scene has echoes of the young Athanasius, at almost exactly the same age, standing beside his own uncle Alexander, Bishop of Alexandria, some 87 years earlier. Like Athanasius at the Council of Nicaea in 325, Cyril played no part in that Synod (he later wrote that he was a 'bystander') but would come to succeed his uncle in that same prominent bishopric.[34]

Theophilus died in October 412 and a race began to find his replacement. The Archdeacon Timothy was the preference of many, but Cyril was the favourite of others, and rioting and other street disturbances ensued until, three days after Theophilus has passed away, Cyril was elected and enthroned, aged around 35, on 17th October 412.[35]

Cyril the New Bishop

Every overview of Cyril's life will reference several controversies that apparently rocked the first years of his episcopate: his closure of churches of the Novationist sect, simmering tension and then violent clashes between Christian and Jewish residents of Alexandria, and the murder of the philosopher Hypatia. These are entangled with what seems to be a long and complicated quarrel with Alexandria's Urban Prefect, Orestes. After these, the next available 'headline' in Cyril's life is the dispute with Nestorius that came to define him, so it would be all too easy to draw the conclusion that he was a man uniquely given to

---

33. Cf. Matthew R. Crawford, 'Reconsidering the Relationship between (Pseudo-) Didymus's *De Trinitate* and Cyril of Alexandria's *Contra Julianum*', *Journal of Theological Studies* 71 (April 2020): 236–57.

34. Cyril, Letter 33. English translation used: John I. McEnerney, *St Cyril of Alexandria: Letters 1–50, Fathers of the Church* 76 (Washington DC: Catholic University of American Press, 2007), 131.

35. Socrates Scholasticus, Eccl. Hist. 7.7.

conflict and intrigue. These events all deserve our attention, but we must also keep in mind that Cyril was largely busy being a pastor through this time. Each year, the patriarchs of Alexandria traditionally sent a 'festal letter' to their clergy and the wider flock. These letters announced the start of the season of Lent and published the date of *Pascha* (Easter) for that year. They also served as a 'State of the Nation' address to the faithful, dealing with theological and catechetical issues in an accessible way. From Cyril's 32 years in post, only three of his festal letters are not extant and translated. This means that, quite apart from revealing the theological foundations that would support Cyril in the well-known work he would later do, they give us a picture of his ministry in more general terms.[36]

Cyril was a prolific writer and, if he had ever imagined himself becoming famous for anything, it might have been as a biblical exegete and commentator. We do not know exactly the timeline of all his works, but it is likely during this early period that he wrote a series of sermons on the Pentateuch (The *Glaphyra*) and commentaries on the book of Isaiah, the Minor Prophets, and John's and Luke's Gospels. Beside these, we have fragments of his commentaries on Kings, Psalms, Proverbs, Song of Songs, Jeremiah, Ezekiel, Daniel, Matthew, Romans, and 1 and 2 Corinthians. Cyril's theological works from the first 16 or so years of his episcopate include a treatise on true worship (*De Adoratione*) and books on the doctrine of the Trinity (*The Thesaurus, Dialogues on the Trinity*). The dawning of the Nestorian controversy (in 428) then seems to become the great theme of his writing. Apart from *Against Julian* (a critique of paganism in response to the Emperor Julian written in the late 430s) and the festal letters, his output centred on tackling Nestorianism, and included *On the Unity of Christ* and writings against Nestorius and

---

36. O'Keefe, *St. Cyril of Alexandria: Festal Letters* 1-12, 3-12. The Festal Letters of Cyril have long been available in French thanks to Évieux (SC vol. 372) and Arragon and Burns (SC vol. 434), but the English edition above is the most recent and includes an excellent introduction from John O'Keefe.

his teachers. Cyril's commentary on Hebrews may also belong in this later stage given some of its language and themes.[37] This commentary has generally been extant only in small fragments, but the discovery in 2020 of a fifteenth century Armenian manuscript has brought far more of its contents to light.[38] All this writing, along with pastoring his clergy, will have been the lion's share of his daily work and routine.

Nevertheless, it is true that almost immediately on becoming bishop, Cyril flexed his muscles. First, he cracked down on the Novationists. Named for Bishop Novatian (c. 200-258) by most Christians, this faction referred to themselves as *katharoi*, 'the pure', because they considered the practices of other Christians to be very much second-rate and rather grimy. They looked with particular disgust on those who had turned away from the faith under persecution, refusing them communion and a second chance, even if they exhibited sincere repentance. These beliefs are anticipated to some degree in the first century work *The Shepherd of Hermas*, and Cyril's confiscation of their buildings is mirrored by the church's treatment of the very similar Donatist movement in the West around the same time. Such spiritual superiority undermined the gospel both by withholding grace from sinners and leaving the 'pure' in unhealthy denial of their own failure. Theophilus had been relatively gentle with

37. Cyril, *Commentaries on Romans, 1-2 Corinthians, and Hebrews*, ed. Joel C. Elowsky, trans. David R. Maxwell, Ancient Christian Texts (Downers Grove: Inter-Varsity Press, 2022), 23; Hakob Keoseyan, *Meknut'iwn ebrayets'wots' t'ght'oyn = Commentary on the letter to the Hebrews*, ed. D. Tsaghikyan, trans. Khachʻik Grigoryan (Yerevan: Ankyunacar Publishing, 2021), 10-12. Cyril's attack in Oration 1 in the Hebrews commentary on those who 'divide the Christ' because 'they want to be worshippers of their friends' is a clear attack on Nestorius and his reliance on Theodore (*Commentary on Hebrews*, 41).

38. For the fragmentary commentary, see Cyril, *Commentaries on Romans, 1-2 Corinthians, and Hebrews*, ed. Joel C. Elowsky, trans. David R. Maxwell, Ancient Christian Texts (Downers Grove: IVP Academic, 2022); for an English translation of the recently discovered 15th century Armenian manuscript, see Cyril and Hakob Keoseyan, *Meknut'iwn ebrayets'wots' t'ght'oyn = Commentary on the letter to the Hebrews*, ed. D. Tsaghikyan, trans. Khachʻik Grigoryan (Yerevan: Ankyunacar Publishing, 2021).

the group but Cyril, perhaps looking to assert himself, wanted to outdo his uncle in ridding the church of beliefs that did such damage.[39]

Orestes became Urban Prefect of Alexandria three years after Cyril's election. His role as the representative of the emperor was to maintain law and order and to administrate the government of Roman Egypt. Upon taking this role, he was immediately unhappy with the power and influence Cyril enjoyed but, as the new kid on the block, was unable to alter the dynamic in any meaningful way at first. Beyond the long-established power of the patriarchs of the city, the Alexandrian church was growing in influence in society more widely.[40] It owned a fleet of ships and operated a trade in wheat, wine, and handcrafts; it collected taxes and rents from land; it had a steady income from legacies and pilgrimage fees at shrines. The church had a significant economic and civic infrastructure, enabling it to build hospitals and chapels.[41] On his election, Cyril would have moved into the Caesareum – a large colonnaded harbourside compound serving as the patriarch's official residence, boasting a library and several administrative staff and offices. He also inherited Alexandria's *parabalani*. These were guilds of 'nurses' or 'hospital porters' in many ancient cities, originally tasked by the church with the care of the sick and the burial of the dead. By Cyril's time in Alexandria, the *parabalani* was a brotherhood of 500 or 600 and doubled as the bishop's bodyguards and private military troop.[42]

It seems that, by the time Orestes arrived on the scene, Cyril had already been at work to expand the temporal and civil clout of his office, even more than had his uncle had before him. His success here was the cause of some jealousy and suspicion from

---

39. Évieux, *Lettres Festales*, I–VI, 28.

40. For more on what Haas calls the 'growing ascendency of the Christian community' in the city during this time, see his *Alexandria in Late Antiquity*, 9.

41. See Évieux, *Lettres Festales*, I–VI, 34–41.

42. See Haas, *Alexandria in Late Antiquity*, 237; 314-6 for an excellent study on the *parabalani*.

Orestes. The relationship between the two men was consistently marked by lack of communication, mutual mistrust, and envy. The feud between them was a catalyst for the storms that blew through Cyril's first years as bishop. The earliest and most reliable source for all this is the *Ecclesiastical History of Socrates Scholasticus* (380-439) who was directly contemporaneous with all the events. Socrates appears to be no great fan of Cyril's and was possibly a Novationist, or at least sympathetic to that group.[43] He tries, though, to be even-handed in his history, and it is his telling we will follow below.[44] He is aware of the political subtleties, and he is capable of placing events in that context. There are some later sources with material on Cyril's early years which seem to have more obvious biases one way or another and are significantly further away from the personalities, events, and geography than Socrates.

Cyril, Orestes, and Alexandria's Jews

The first clash between Cyril and Orestes was over relations between Alexandria's Jewish and Christian populations. The Jewish community regularly held dances and other entertainments on the Sabbath, frequently leading to public disorder as Christians and Jews clashed in the streets. Orestes decided to regulate the shows and published an edict in the theatre one day when many of the Jews had gathered there. Among the crowd, Hierax, a Christian man, was spotted very visibly and noisily signalling his pleasure at the public reprimand to the Jews. The audience at the theatre – and Orestes' troops – assumed he was a spy, sent there to cause disruption. He was beaten up by the crowd, arrested, and tortured while the people looked on.

---

43. Theresa Urbainczyk, *Socrates of Constantinople: Historian of Church and State* (Ann Arbor, MI: University of Michigan Press, 1997), 26-29.

44. Socrates, *Eccl. Hist.*, 7.13-15.

Instead of taking the matter up with Orestes, Cyril sent for the Jewish leaders and angrily demanded an end to the mistreatment of Christians, as though the episode were their fault. The confrontation only made things worse. In the middle of the night shortly afterwards, a Jewish group sent runners through the streets shouting that the Church of Alexander was burning down, drawing local Christians to the site in panic. Once they had arrived to discover no fire, they were ambushed, and several of them were killed. The following morning, a furious Christian mob gathered at the cathedral. Led by Cyril (who again took matters into his own hands rather than deferring to Orestes' civil power), they proceeded to the synagogues of the perpetrators, vandalising their buildings and chasing the suspects out of the city. This sparked wider-scale looting and rioting. For his part, Orestes was rightly incensed that Cyril had taken it upon himself to punish and evict Alexandrian citizens and so had precipitated yet another wave of criminal activity. He wrote an official report to the emperor to complain, and Cyril also wrote his own letter in defence.

Socrates implies that Cyril, in his capacity as bishop, was able at this time to banish all the Jews from the city single-handedly. This is a serious claim and tends to invite comparisons with medieval expulsions of Jews from major cities or later pogroms, driven by ethnic or religious hatred. The claim is almost certainly an exaggeration on Socrates' part.[45] Harassment of Jews was illegal under Emperor Theodosius II, and Cyril would not have been able to do something like this without significant consequences.[46] In any case, a Jewish population is in evidence in Alexandria long into the sixth century, continuing to be

---

45.   Ross Shepard Kraemer, *The Mediterranean Diaspora in Late Antiquity: What Christianity Cost the Jews* (Oxford: Oxford University Press, 2020), 188–239.

46.   Pierre Périchon and Pierre Maraval, eds. *Socrate de Constantinople, Histoire Écclesiastique, Livre VII*. SC 506 (Paris: Les Éditions du Cerf, 2007), 52–53n2.

influential and invaluable in its culture and industry.[47] While it is tragically true that anti-Judaism and antisemitism have plagued the Church at various times in its history, it would be a stretch to read it here in any direct sense. In many ways, neither group emerges looking very honourable from the tit-for-tat violence. The passions of the Alexandrians of all stripes were roused on several occasions as the city's Christians, pagans, and Jews reacted variously to their changing relationships to one another.[48]

Whatever the detail, from this time on, Cyril and Orestes were at loggerheads. The next stage in this saga, Socrates says, is that five hundred Nitrian monks of 'a very fiery disposition' soon came to Alexandria in a show of support for Cyril and, recognising Orestes in his chariot, shouted abuse and threw stones at him. One monk, Ammonius, scored a direct hit on Orestes' head and drew blood, sending his bodyguards scurrying away. Orestes had Ammonius captured and tortured so severely that he died. Cyril's response was to honour Ammonius with the title 'the Admirable' and declare him a martyr for the faith. Socrates says that this move was not necessarily well received by 'sober-minded' Christians who could see that Ammonius was not so much a martyr as foolish and rash.[49] Again, both Orestes and Cyril submitted conflicting reports to the emperor, each stubbornly holding his own line.

The Murder of Hypatia

Perhaps nothing has harmed Cyril's reputation more than a vicious murder that was committed, apparently by a mob of

---

47. See J. David Cassel, *Cyril of Alexandria and the Science of the Grammarians: A Study in the Setting, Purpose, and Emphasis in Cyril's Commentary on Isaiah* (PhD dissertation, University of Virginia, 1992); Robert L. Wilken, *Judaism and the Early Christian Mind: A Study of Cyril of Alexandria's Exegesis and Theology* (New Haven: Yale University Press, 1971), 57; John McGuckin, *St Cyril of Alexandria and the Christological Controversy* (Leiden: Brill, 1994), 12.

48. See Haas, *Alexandria in Late Antiquity*, 8–9.

49. Socrates, *Eccl. Hist.* 7.14.

Christians, in Lent 415, just three years into his episcopate. It is worth delving into the rather ugly details and establishing Cyril's connection to it. The victim was Hypatia: a famous and well-loved figure in Alexandrian society. She was a philosopher in the Neoplatonic tradition, an astronomer and mathematician, and her teaching was of such quality that students came from around the world to listen to her lectures. She was part of Alexandria's social elite, enjoying personal friendships with civic leaders, and easily recognised about town in her philosopher's cloak.[50]

Hypatia was a female academic in a world otherwise rather dominated by men, so, even in her own lifetime, had devolved something of a mythos. According to one early source (Damascius), she was 'so beautiful and shapely' that one young man in her class fell in love with her and, 'unable to control himself... openly showed her a sign of his infatuation.' At this sight, Hypatia (reputedly a lifelong virgin) chastely 'gathered rags that had been stained during her period' and, showing them to him, warned her student, 'This is what you love, young man, and it isn't beautiful!' So amazed and ashamed was her admirer that 'he experienced a change of heart and went away a better man.'[51] Long beyond her lifetime, though, Hypatia has been adopted as a symbol of the feminine purity of ancient paganism and even a kind of proto-feminist, whose innocent wisdom was snuffed out by the might of an intolerant and patriarchal Christianity. For modern Western historians, there has been an almost irresistible

50. For more on Hypatia, see Peter Brown, *Power and Persuasion in Late Antiquity: Towards a Christian Empire* (Madison: University of Wisconsin Press, 1992); Pierre Chuvin, *A Chronicle of the Last Pagans* (Harvard: Harvard University Press, 1990); Maria Dzielska, *Hypatia of Alexandria* (London: CUP, 1995); Edward Watts, *The Murder of Hypatia: Acceptable or Unacceptable Violence?* (London: Routledge, 2006); Michael A. B. Deakin, *Hypatia of Alexandria: Mathematician and Martyr* (Amherst: Prometheus, 2007).

51. Damascius, *Life of Isidore*, trans. Jeremiah Reedy in *The Life of Hypatia in the Suda*, Alexandria 2 (Grand Rapids: Phanes Press, 1993), 57–58.

urge to implicate Cyril in her death as a symbol of just such a cruel and intolerant religion.[52]

The most well-known example of all this is perhaps Edward Gibbon's magisterial *Decline and Fall of the Roman Empire* (1772–1789). Christianity was, for Gibbon, the primary cause of the downfall of ancient pagan civilisation, and Hypatia's tragic femininity ('in the bloom of beauty') is emblematic of its loss. Her murder is the zenith of a brazen Christian campaign against all these noble qualities, inspired by the muscle of Cyril, a tyrannical 'episcopal warrior', usurping his way to power and commanding bands of fanatics drawn from Alexandria's underclass. Hypatia's murder is set in religious, almost cultic, terms as 'the sacrifice of a virgin' at Cyril's behest.[53] Hypatia looks like nothing short of a martyr for paganism, philosophy, and femininity. Gibbon has certainly shaped the popular imagination of both Hypatia and Cyril. His influence stretches from Charles Kingsley's 1853 anti-Catholic novel, *Hypatia*, through Carl Sagan's 1980 documentary TV series, *Cosmos*, to the 2009 film *Agora* by Alejandro Amenábar and Mateo Gil.[54] It is all very worthy and poetic – but nonsense all the same.

Socrates gives us crucial detail about the events and their most probable cause.[55] The circumstances of Hypatia's murder are unquestionably horrific. She was apparently ambushed in her carriage one day and dragged to the Caesareum (an ancient temple converted into a church), where she was stripped naked

---

52. Edward Gibbon, as we will see below, is perhaps the most influential purveyor of this perspective. He was probably influenced by John Toland's furious 1735 pamphlet on Hypatia. John Toland, *Hypatia* (London: Cooper, Reeve, and Sympson, 1753). See also Maria Dzielska, *Hypatia of Alexandria* (London: CUP, 1995).

53. Edward Gibbon, *The Decline and Fall of the Roman Empire* [Abridgement: D. M. Low] (London: Book Club Associates, 1960), chapter 47.

54. In the film, Hypatia's talents are somewhat overestimated (she is shown anticipating heliocentrism) while Christians are cleverly depicted as swarming locusts, dressed in black, fanatically looting venerable pagan sites. It is an entirely fictional piece.

55. The following is drawn from Chapters 13–15 of book 7 of Socrates' *Ecclesiastical History.*

and hacked to death with broken tiles. Her remains were burned nearby. Those responsible were Christians (even if they were such in name only) and their ringleader was a layman named Peter. Socrates writes that the murder brought 'the greatest opprobrium' on Cyril and on the Alexandrian church, because 'nothing can be further from the spirit of Christianity than the allowance of massacres, fights, and transactions of that sort.' He is undoubtedly correct.

Why was Hypatia killed and was Cyril to blame in some way?
Damascius' *Life of Isidore* directly implicates Cyril. This text is preserved in the *Suda*, a tenth-century Byzantine encyclopaedia of the ancient Mediterranean world. Cyril was wandering past Hypatia's house and was overcome with envy on seeing a great crowd of people (and even horses!), all eager to meet her. He immediately began to plan the most gruesome murder he could possibly imagine and sent a band of thugs to 'cut her down'.[56] There are several issues with Damascius' story which might cause us to question his reliability. First, Hypatia is very much idealised as the pure, innocent, and virginal victim, while Cyril comes over as a kind of Alexandrian Fagin with stereotypically villainous henchmen. It is hard not to sense that 'goodies and baddies' are a little too cartoonish to be taken seriously.[57] Second, there is no explanation of why Cyril might suddenly have felt quite so threatened by a woman who had been famous in the city since he was a teenager. By the time Cyril became bishop, Hypatia had already been teaching in Alexandria for 22 years, so it seems quite unlikely that either could have imagined some kind of competition for profile.[58] It seems that Orestes

---

56. Damascius, *Life of Isidore*, trans. Jeremiah Reedy in *The Life of Hypatia in the Suda*, Alexandria 2 (Grand Rapids: Phanes Press, 1993), 57–58.

57. See Edward Watts, *The Murder of Hypatia: Acceptable or Unacceptable Violence?* (London: Routledge, 2006), 337.

58. A point made by P. Chuvin, *A Chronicle of the Last Pagans* (Harvard: Harvard University Press, 1990), 89.

had apparently granted to Hypatia the privilege of *parhésia*, a local freedom of speech privilege with implied access to the sources of political power and Damascius may have had this in mind as a motive for murder.[59] We might wonder, though, whether Cyril's position afforded him any less opportunity to rub shoulders with the great and the good. A third issue is that Damascius' material on Cyril's personal jealousy and campaign against Hypatia is entirely absent from Socrates' much earlier account of the murder, and its origin is completely unexplained.

It may be that Damascius' story is no more than a pagan gloss on the events added 130 years after the fact to link Cyril to the crime.[60] But this is where a fixation with a 'Christians versus pagans' narrative could lead us astray. It is sometimes read into Damascius' account when it is not really there. Jeremiah Reedy's 1993 translation of Damascius rather ups the ante on this point with the insertion of some square brackets by way of interpretation when he speaks about 'Cyril, bishop of the opposition sect [*i.e., Christianity*]'.[61] Reedy's explanation of the word 'sect' (αἵρεσιν, 'choice, opinion') to refer to Cyril's religion assumes that Damascius is referring to the opposition of *Christianity and paganism* and so flavours the murder with a twist of religious extremism. Damascius was the last head of the Neoplatonic Academy in Athens and watched its decline in the face of growing Christianity. It would be tempting to imagine that he had cooked up a juicy tale of a Christian bishop's jealous murder of a great pagan thinker as a perfect piece of propaganda. It is unlikely, though, that this is what Damascius was trying to do. The word 'sect' can refer to any persuasion or faction in a given conflict and, since Damascius does not mention religious

---

59. See Lionel Wickham, *Cyril of Alexandria: Select Letters* (Oxford: OUP, 1983), 8, and Peter Brown, *Power and Persuasion in Late Antiquity: Towards a Christian Empire* (Madison: University of Wisconsin Press, 1992), 116.

60. See Watts, *Murder*, 333–337; McGuckin, *St Cyril of Alexandria and the Christological Controversy* (Leiden: Brill, 1994), 14.

61. Reedy, *Hypatia*, 57 (emphasis mine).

concerns at all in his section on Hypatia, we should probably prefer the more general definition of the word. The 'sects' he mentions are simply the *political factions* of Orestes and Cyril. He is not trying to depict the murder as an act of religious terrorism. In fact, Damascius seems to think the murderers' professed religion ought to have *prevented* them from acting as they did, rather than *motivate* them: he complains that they did not 'fear divine punishment' as they brutalised Hypatia. This reading is perfectly in line with Socrates and means that Damascius only adds to the earlier source his own tale of Cyril's personal involvement and envy. This is an embellishment seemingly plucked out of thin air and nearly impossible to demonstrate, especially by someone born nearly half a century after the event.

One later account, that of John of Nikiu, in the late seventh century has tended to pour petrol on the flames.[62] Writing 250 years or so after Hypatia's murder, John, a Monophysite bishop who would have held Cyril in the highest regard, attempts to salvage from Socrates' book a kind of 'hero' status for Cyril.[63] He invents a backstory in which Hypatia was a 'magician' in possession of 'Satanic wiles' and Orestes was one of many enchanted by her malevolent power. John says that, after the murder, Cyril was hailed a 'new Theophilus', because he had 'destroyed the last remains of paganism in the city'. Clearly, the dispatch of such a terrible and manipulative witch could only be right and proper, so if Cyril was involved at all, he deserves nothing but applause. Beside leaning on Socrates, John probably drew on rumour and innuendo – whether pro- or anti-Cyril – and tried to spin it for his own ends to make Cyril look (in his

---

62. John of Nikiu, *Chronicle* in: Robert Henry Charles, *The Chronicle of John (c. 690A.D.), Coptic Bishop of Nikiu: Being a History of Egypt Before and During the Arab Conquest* (Amsterdam 1981; reprint of 1916), 84.87–103.

63. See Michael A. B. Deakin, *Hypatia of Alexandria: Mathematician and Martyr* (Amherst: Prometheus, 2007), 46.

eyes at least) like a great champion of faith.[64] He is by no means a reliable witness.

In Socrates, though, there is no mention of Cyril at the scene nor of him covertly pulling the strings. There is none of Damascius' 'Cyril the villain' or John's 'Cyril the crusader'. Given Cyril's treatment of the Novationists, Socrates possessed both motive and opportunity to paint Cyril in the bleakest terms when it came to Hypatia, should he have wished. In the last book of his *Ecclesiastical History*, Cyril is clearly meant to be a malevolent figure: John McGuckin says that Socrates deliberately 'telescopes' together the various tempestuous events of Cyril's early episcopate to present him as a poor leader.[65] Socrates could easily have stained Cyril's hands with Hypatia's blood. Instead, there is every indication that he deals with Cyril quite fairly in this sorry episode. The dispute he had nurtured with Orestes contributed to an atmosphere of violence and uproar in the city. When 'calumnious' rumours sprang up that Orestes enjoyed a close relationship with Hypatia, and that she was the sole reason for his hostility to Cyril, her fate was sealed. The mob who attacked her had been 'hurried away by a fierce and bigoted zeal' rather than by orders from their bishop, making her the sad victim of the 'political jealousy which at the time prevailed'.[66]

There is no reason to suppose that Cyril was directly involved in Hypatia's murder, whether sanctioning it or even welcoming it. There is no evidence that his *parabalani* had anything to do with it, as is sometimes suggested.[67] We might conclude, with John McGuckin, that when it comes to much scholarship in the modern era surrounding this event, Cyril has been 'caricatured, lampooned, and even accused of misogynistic murder (without

---

64. See Watts, *The Murder of Hypatia*, 340.

65. John McGuckin, *Saint Cyril of Alexandria and the Christological Controversy* (Leiden: Brill, 1994), 7.

66. Socrates, *Hist. Eccl.*, 7.15.

67. See Haas, *Alexandria in Late Antiquity*, 314.

sufficient scholarly basis in my opinion – though that has not seemed to rein in academics' relish for lurid details whether real or imaginary).'[68] Socrates' account of Cyril's connection to the murder is certainly critical and negative, but it is honest and nuanced enough not to throw him under the bus. Like Socrates, we might characterise Cyril as both bullish and negligent. Hypatia was the victim of a political feud that got very far out of hand, and in which Cyril had been an enthusiastic participant. He was unable – perhaps unwilling – to control the monks and the mobs; too immature, perhaps, to handle the events and the climate of aggression, and so culpable, indirectly, in a bloody and tragic killing.[69]

Learning to Lead

Today, we tend to blanch easily at stories of violence, armed monks, and anathemas in the early church, yet the ancient world was well accustomed to this way of dealing with social or philosophical debate. Gregory of Nyssa famously wrote on his arrival in Constantinople:

> The whole city is full of it, the squares, the market places, the cross-roads, the alleyways; old-clothes men, money changers, food sellers: they are all busy arguing. If you ask someone to give you change, he philosophizes about the Begotten and the Unbegotten; if you inquire about the price of a loaf, you are told by way of reply that the Father is greater and the Son inferior; if you ask "Is my bath ready?" the attendant answers that the Son was made out of nothing.[70]

---

68. John A. McGuckin, "Cyril of Alexandria: Bishop and Pastor," in *The Theology of St Cyril of Alexandria: A Critical Appreciation*, ed. Thomas G. Weinandy and Daniel A. Keating (London: T&T Clark, 2003), 205.

69. See Matthew R. Crawford, 'Cyril of Alexandria's Renunciation of Religious Violence' in *Church History* 92, no. 1 (2003): 1–21, for a balance analysis of Cyril's contribution to the violent climate at the time.

70. Gregory of Nyssa, On the Deity of the Son [PG xlvi, 557b], quoted in Timothy Ware, *The Orthodox Church* (London: Penguin Books, 1997), 35.

Clearly, matters of theological importance were taken up with vigour by the laity, and it was not uncommon for feelings to run high, especially in major cities with very diverse populations. Reading Socrates' account of Cyril's first few years in office, the clear impression is that Cyril bears much of the blame for the conflict with Orestes that spilled over so sadly into Alexandria's public life. Socrates sees Cyril's episcopate as the moment at which the Alexandrian bishops began to trespass further beyond their sacerdotal functions and into secular matters than before.

Despite all this, there are signs that Cyril was not completely ham-fisted while trying to find his way as a young leader. It seems that, in the early months of their feud, Cyril made efforts at reconciliation with Orestes. Having explained his side of the events surrounding the street violence, Cyril extended the Gospel book for Orestes to kiss – hoping that they might find some harmony in a symbol of their common faith. The prefect pointedly refused and persisted in what Socrates calls 'implacable hostility against' Cyril. Having initially rushed to praise Ammonius (the monk who had pelted Orestes), Cyril seems to have realised the childishness of his reaction and quietly dropped the matter, attempting to de-escalate the situation.[71] In his festal letter of 423, Cyril reflects on Ephesians 4:32, 'Be kind to one another, tenderhearted, forgiving one another, as God in Christ forgave you.' He writes, with some self-awareness in his Festal Letter 11:

> It is necessary, then, beloved, that we also practice forbearance, hastening to follow in the footsteps of the tranquillity which is in the Master of all. And let us give prudent consideration to the following: human failings are countless, and there is no occasion which is free of our pettiness. But if, whenever that occurs, we are going to get upset seriously and enter into

---

71. Socrates, *Hist. Eccl.*, 7.13–14.

disputes with those who have grieved us, our whole life will be
spent in bitterness and distress.[72]

This is not the well-worn caricature of Cyril the power-hungry
tyrant. There is no question that Cyril managed his political
power poorly at the start of his episcopate and struggled to
find his feet as a leader in an especially volatile city. But, to his
credit, he seems to recognise in himself the danger that Cyril
the biblical exegete and popular pastor was in danger of eclipse
by 'Cyril the cage-stage hothead'. The young bishop apparently
received wise counsel that helped him cool off and mellow as a
leader, enabling him to emerge as a skilled politician and careful
strategist. Matthew R. Crawford has argued persuasively that
Cyril appears to have changed his rhetoric – possibly because of
the murder of Hypatia – and clearly disavowed religious violence
at least three times in writings.[73]

The mature Cyril evidently learned how to direct his spikiness.
By the time of his famous confrontation with Nestorius in 428,
he had learned how to fight the right battles. He knew how to
play his hand with tact and shrewdness. So much the better, for
the stakes were far higher to Cyril than politics and personal
status. The controversy that was about to erupt in the Church
went to the heart of the things Cyril had already begun to make
central to his ministry of teaching and preaching: the nature of
God, the person and work of Christ, and the salvation offered
in the gospel.

---

72. O'Keefe, *Festal Letters* 1–12, 208.

73. Crawford, 'Renunciation of Religious Violence,' 1–21. These are, it seems, writings
     from after the time of Hypatia's murder.

2

THE NESTORIAN CONTROVERSY

The defining chapter of Cyril's life – and the great test of his theology – was to begin in 428 when a priest called Nestorius was elected to be Archbishop of Constantinople. The two men would soon clash in dramatic fashion over their opposite understandings of Christ's divinity and humanity. It is this controversy that has become synonymous with Cyril, and which has left his stamp on the whole of Christian theology in the centuries since. As Lionel Wickham has written,

> The patristic understanding of the Incarnation owes more to Cyril of Alexandria than any other individual theologian. The classic picture of Christ the God-man, as it is delineated in the formulae of the Church from the Council of Chalcedon onwards, and as it has been presented to the heart in the liturgies and hymns, is the picture Cyril persuaded Christians was the true, the only credible, Christ. All subsequent Christology has proceeded, and must proceed, by way of interpretation or criticism of this picture.[1]

---

1.   Lionel Wickham, ed., *Cyril of Alexandria: Select Letters* (Oxford: Clarendon Press, 1983), xi.

Lighting the Flames

Finding a new archbishop for Constantinople was always a turbulent, political affair – and it was no different in 428 when various pressure groups each clamoured to set up their own man for the job. This was a powerful position in the Church not only because Constantinople was known as the 'new Rome' and the hub of the empire in the East, but because the archbishop there had increasing influence over the bishops of other local towns and cities.[2]

Nestorius, from Antioch in Syria, was seen as the dark horse candidate and not many expected him to be selected. It seems that a personal recommendation from John, Bishop of Antioch, may have sealed the deal. Nestorius and John had grown up together and John had praised his friend's ability as a preacher (especially his excellent voice) and his life of exemplary discipline and asceticism. Whatever the ins and outs, choosing Nestorius for the top job seemed to short-circuit some of the factional politicking and infighting, and was seen to be the smart option for peace and quiet. As Nestorius was enthroned in April 428, the imperial court could not have imagined just how wrong it had been.[3]

Conflict and controversy immediately followed wherever Nestorius went. He was known to be a dogmatic personality: scrupulous about details, propriety, and process. He was apparently not a man of subtlety or compromise. In his first sermon as archbishop, he directly addressed the emperor, Theodosius II:

---

2. Five big cities all vied for supremacy in the Roman Empire at this time. Rome was the old political centre and Constantinople its newer (more explicitly Christian) rival. Alexandria and Antioch were the competing academic hotbeds, and Jerusalem never lost its magic as the birthplace of the Christian faith. For more on Constantinople and its importance, a good starting point is John Julius Norwich's three volume history, *Byzantium* (London, Penguin: 1988–95).

3. Socrates, *Hist. Eccl.* 7.29.

Give me, my prince, the earth purged of heretics, and I will give you heaven as a recompense. Assist me in destroying heretics, and I will assist you in vanquishing the Persians.[4]

Socrates judged Nestorius not to be especially bright, but 'violent and vainglorious'. He 'burst forth into such vehemence without being able to contain himself for even the shortest space of time' and 'before he had tasted the water of the city', threw himself into persecuting various groups and throwing around the insult 'heretic' quite freely.[5] Nestorius promptly ordered the demolition of a chapel belonging to a congregation of Arians who, on seeing their building being destroyed, set it alight—a fire that spread to surrounding buildings, devastating the whole area. This episode earned Nestorius the nickname 'Torchie', not only from his enemies but also his own monks and clergy, who could see he was liable to burn much else to the ground.[6] And indeed, Nestorius fell out with just about everyone in Constantinople.

He deeply offended Pulcheria, the formidable sister of the emperor, possibly in the first state church service he conducted at Easter, when he refused to give her communion. The source for the story may not be entirely reliable: a letter to one Cosmas, purportedly from supporters of Nestorius. It records that Pulcheria had been accustomed to receiving the sacrament alongside her brother in the sanctuary, otherwise strictly reserved only for clergy, her royal status and a vow of celibacy satisfying Nestorius' predecessors that she could enjoy this honour. But he attempted to bar her way and she apparently protested: 'Let me enter... Have I not given birth to God?' (a comparison of herself with the Virgin Mary; an argument that her virginal purity should admit her to the holy place). Nestorius was supposed to

---

4. Socrates, *Hist. Eccl.* 7.29.

5. Socrates, *Hist. Eccl.* 7.29.

6. 'Torchie' is John McGuckin's rendering of the Greek *'purkaia'* in Socrates, Hist. Eccl. 7.29. The word is something like the equivalent of 'firebrand'. See McGuckin, *The Christological Controversy*, 24.

have snapped, 'You have given birth to Satan!" and chased her away. Events are unlikely to have unfolded this way – not least because Nestorius was not immediately deposed or executed![7] Nevertheless, there is a grain of truth in the description of the clash between the two.

Nestorius was deeply rude about Pulcheria in his writings some years later, saying quite explicitly that she was 'a woman corrupted of men' (i.e., not the virgin she claimed to be) and that he refused to be the 'celebrant of the sacrifice' (the Eucharist) for her. He says he has generally tried to 'keep silence about and hide everything else about her own little self' although she had fought against him constantly.[8] McGuckin wonders whether Nestorius had a problem with 'independent women', a number of whom he riled in Constantinople.[9] One wealthy and venerable woman of the city, Eliana the wife of Damarios the praetorian prefect, claimed to have had an angelic visitation three years before Nestorius' arrival. The angel had warned her that a troublesome bishop was on his way and that she should 'take good care and do not receive communion from him'. She obeyed this command, refused to let Nestorius into her home (though he tried to visit several times), and stayed away from church while he was present. One day, though, her interest piqued by reports of blasphemies in his preaching, she went along to church to find out the truth. Listening to Nestorius' sermon, and 'inflamed with divine zeal', she remembered the vision and shouted out from the balcony, 'Cursed be you, Antichrist!'[10]

---

7.   See Stephen J. Shoemaker, *Mary in Early Christian Faith and Devotion* (New Haven: Yale, 2016), 210–214.

8.   Nestorius, *Book of Heraclides*, I.iii.

9.   McGuckin, *The Christological Controversy*, 27–28. Thomas Graumann is less certain about this conclusion (see his 'General Introduction' in Richard Price, *The Council of Ephesus 431: Documents and Proceedings*, Translated Texts for Historians [Liverpool: Liverpool University Press, 2020], 24–25.).

10.   John Rufus Plerophoria, 36, in *Patrologia Orientalis* 8, 81–82.

These little cameos demonstrate something of Nestorius' character, perhaps, but they also resonate with the most serious controversy he caused which not only outraged the people of Constantinople but rippled out through the whole church. It involved his opinions on another of Christendom's very well-regarded women: Mary, the mother of Jesus.

Something about Mary

It was common in the early church's liturgy and in personal prayer to use a range of phrases which expressed something of the mystery of the incarnation. Christians would speak about 'God wrapped in swaddling bands' at the nativity or that 'God the Word died on the cross' at Easter.[11] These phrases were designed to be surprising and to pull the worshipper up short. They cause a collision in our imaginations: that the one who came as a helpless baby and was later crucified for us was none other than God the Son Himself. This was the key conviction of the Nicene fathers in 325 when they said that the one who was 'homoousios' (one being) with the Father is the very same one who 'came down' and was born, died, risen, and ascended 'for us men and for our salvation'. Our very salvation rests on the identity of Jesus Christ as 'one Lord' in both His divine and human natures.[12]

Along with these popular phrases was the name *Theotokos*; a title for Mary which means 'God-bearer' (or, sometimes 'Mother of God'). It was that title that caused Nestorius to go to war. To modern evangelical ears, the idea of having a special title for Mary (let alone one that calls her the mother of God) can make us a little uncomfortable: it seems like later Roman Catholic veneration of Mary, and we tend to think Nestorius may have

---

11. McGuckin, *The Christological Controversy*, 151-52.

12. For more on the theology of the Nicene Creed, see Donald Fairbairn and Ryan Reeves, *The Story of Creeds and Confessions* (Grand Rapids: Baker Academic, 2019), 48-79.

had a point if he did not like it.[13] However, along with the other liturgical turns of phrase above, the title was being used primarily as a reminder that Mary's baby was indeed God the Word made flesh (John 1:14). The title bequeathed to Mary was a *Christological* confession rather than a comment about Mary. Squaring up to the influence of Arianism, which denied the divinity of the Son, the Church had incorporated into its worship the regular affirmation that the child born of Mary was God Himself. As Matthew 1:23 says, quoting the prophet Isaiah, 'the virgin shall conceive and bear (*tiktō*) a son, and they shall call his name "Immanuel" (which means, God (*theos*) with us).' The *Theotokos* title was designed to capture both the very normal pregnancy and birth of the baby, and yet the incredible reality of that baby's conception and eternal Personhood. Mary was not the mother of a mere man, however special or important; her child was God, and the church sought to protect this doctrine against sustained attack by using the title *Theotokos*. The question of a growing devotion to Mary and other saints is something we will revisit in a later chapter, but for now it is enough to say that this was not the real reason for the use of the term. Its purpose was to wonder at the identity of Mary's *Son*.

Nestorius had brought a staff team from Antioch with him to his new role in Constantinople. Among them was a presbyter, Anastasius, who preached in church one day, 'Let no one call Mary *Theotokos*: for Mary was but a woman; and it is impossible that God should be born of a woman.' She should, he argued,

---

13. In 1552, John Calvin wrote to a French church in London, responding to their questions about the title for Mary. Clearly some there had strenuously opposed the title with what Calvin calls 'rashness and too much forwardness'. Yet Calvin agonises that, 'to deal with you with brotherly frankness, I cannot conceal that that title being commonly attributed to the Virgin in sermons is disapproved, and, for my own part, I cannot think such language either right, or becoming, or suitable... for it is just as if you were to speak of the blood, of the head, and of the death of God.' Such language, he says, 'can only serve to confirm the ignorant in their superstitions.' John Calvin, Letter 300, in Jules Bonnet, *Letters of John Calvin* vol. 2 (Philadelphia: Presbyterian Board of Publication, 1858), 361–362.

only be referred to as mother of *Jesus the man*.[14] There followed a city-wide outcry which only intensified when the archbishop stepped in to defend his colleague. Towards the end of 428, Nestorius preached a whole sermon series against the use of the title *Theotokos*, preferring to say that Mary could be called *Christotokos*, 'bearer of Christ'.[15] He evidently thought this solution was a move of theological genius which guarded against potential problems with both 'bearer of God' and Anastasius' 'bearer of the man' and so tried to ban both phrases. Some assumed Nestorius likely did not agree with Anastasius but was too proud to admit his appointee was wrong. Others were concerned their new archbishop thought that Jesus was *only* a man, following Paul of Samosata (200-275).[16] The problem with *Christotokos*, as Cyril pointed out later, was that it meant that the son of Mary could be imagined as a different person to the Son of God, and that to worship *that* son of Mary would be to worship a mere man.[17] Many in Constantinople felt that Nestorius had shown his hand, and that any separation between divinity and humanity in Christ was an unacceptable and dangerous theology. Trying to distinguish between God the Son and the son of Mary surely came close to a denial of the Nicene doctrine of 'one Lord Jesus Christ' and struck at the heart of the incarnation.

This made Nestorius quite unpopular in his own diocese. Socrates wrote that, though he was persuaded that Nestorius was no adoptionist, he nevertheless 'seemed scared at the term

---

14. Socrates, *Eccl. Hist.* VI.32.

15. The first of these sermons can be read in Richard A. Norris, *The Christological Controversy*, (Philadelphia: Fortress Press, 1980).

16. Paul, Bishop of Antioch from 260-268, had apparently taught that Christ was a man like one of us but that the Word descended on him at his baptism. This is something close to 'adoptionism' in which Christ is a creature admitted or adopted into a kind of (low level) divinity. See McGuckin, *The Christological Controversy*, 31, 63.

17. Cyril, *Commentary on Hebrews*, 109.

Theotokos, as though it were a terrible phantom' and, proud and quick to speak from his ignorance, he thought himself a better theologian than the ancients.[18] One canny local funded a billboard advertising campaign against Nestorius, characterising him as the new Paul of Samosata.[19] One of Nestorius' own bishops preached a sermon against his views – in his presence – to the applause of the congregation.[20] He increasingly had to endure interruptions and haranguing during his sermons and was known to have ordered the culprits to be roughed up in response.[21] The monks of Constantinople, mocking Nestorius' rather fussy and pompous use of the phrase 'strictly speaking' in all their discussions, darkly joked at his expense: 'If Mary is not, strictly speaking, the Mother of God, then her son is not, strictly speaking, God.'[22] This was exactly the problem.

Cyril Joins the Fray

It seems that Cyril became aware of Nestorius' teachings over the course of 428 as they began to circulate, eventually reaching his own see, some 700 miles south of Constantinople. He quietly watched and waited for some time before deciding that he needed to intervene. Having held his office in Alexandria for around 16 years, he was now a senior figure in the Church. In the Spring of 429, he wrote a letter to the monks of Egypt who had contacted him asking for his advice on the matter. In it, he voiced (without too much nuance) his concern that certain people were 'vomiting out a pile of stupid little words... querying

---

18. Socrates, *Hist. Eccl.* 7.32.

19. The man in question, a lawyer named Eusebius, possibly even made a tour of the city's churches, handing out his tract written against Nestorius. Eusebius was later ordained and served as Bishop of Dorylaeum. See McGuckin, *The Christological Controversy*, 32, and Susan Wessel, 'Nestorius, Mary and Controversy in Cyril's Homily IV (De Maria deipara in Nestorium, CPG 5248)', *Annuarium Historiae Conciliorum* 31 (1999): 1–49.

20. McGuckin, *The Christological Controversy*, 30.

21. McGuckin, *The Christological Controversy*, 33.

22. McGuckin, *The Christological Controversy*, 28.

in their speech whether the holy virgin Mary ought to be called the Mother of God or not.'[23] Despite the explosive opening, the letter goes on to provide a careful and detailed study in the kind of Christology that the *Theotokos* title was meant to embody and safeguard. Cyril sees himself standing in the line of Nicaea and Athanasius as he rejects those who 'divide the one Lord Jesus Christ into two, that is into a man alongside the Word of God the Father' (precisely what he saw Nestorius do).[24] His central concern is clear:

> But if, indeed, Christ is neither truly the Son nor God by nature, but mere man as we are, and an instrument of divinity, we have not been saved by God, have we, but rather since one like ourselves died for us and was raised up by the powers of someone else? How, then was death still destroyed by Christ? ... Because, therefore, he is truly God and king according to nature, and because the crucified one has been called the Lord of glory, how could anyone hesitate to call the Holy Virgin the Mother of God? Adore him as one, without dividing him into two after the union.[25]

Any sense that Jesus is not the Son himself, but can *relate* to him in some way, or was used *by* him, means that our salvation is ruined. Only a Christ who is one person can save us and receive our true worship. This theology was drawn out in a series of further letters from Cyril. The first was his festal letter of 429. That year (*Festal Letter* 17) he took the opportunity to warn against regarding Jesus merely as 'a human being who has borne God'. He must rather be seen *as* God

> who has become a human being, and who, in the economic union, that with his own flesh, has put on the birth from the holy Virgin. The sole Christ and sole Lord may be regarded

---

23. Letter to the Monks of Egypt (Letter 1), translated by McGuckin in *The Christological Controversy*, 246.

24. McGuckin, *The Christological Controversy*, 252.

25. Letter 1 in McEnerney, *St Cyril of Alexandria: Letters 1–50*, 33.

> thus and not otherwise, not as being divided into part human
> being and part God after the ineffable interweaving; even if
> the nature of those which have come together into a union is
> regarded as different, he is received and regarded as being only
> one Son.[26]

What is beginning to emerge here is Cyril's own theology of
the union of divine and human natures or 'realities' in the one
person of Christ, later to be known as 'hypostatic union'. The
one Christ and Lord, crucified and risen, perfectly unites God
and humanity in His one person in what he calls the 'economy'
of His incarnation, for the purpose of our salvation. Although
divinity and humanity are clearly distinct realities, any *division* of
those in Him (such as the idea that Jesus is a man who 'bore' or
carried God the Son) undoes human salvation, since it would
no longer be God Himself who is acting for us in Jesus. We will
examine this theology in more detail in the next chapters – it
is Cyril's great contribution to the Church – but for now it is
enough to see that, after years of biblical commentary, writing,
and pastoring, Cyril was primed and ready.

Cyril and Nestorius soon began correspondence and some
of their letters are preserved – we will turn to them in the next
chapter. The essence of their interaction is that Nestorius dug his
heels in, and Cyril stood his ground. Nestorius clung to a *divisive*
Christology in that it introduced a division in Christ between
the human and divine realities (though it was also divisive in that
it caused division in the Church too). The division was almost
to the point of identifying two parallel 'sons' operating in the
incarnation. Nestorius tended to read through the Gospels and
divide up the actions of Christ between the two realities based
on what was, to his mind, either clearly divine or clearly human.
When the Lord walked on water, Nestorius identified the action

---

26. Festal Letter 17 in Philip R. Amidon and John J. O'Keefe (trans.) *St. Cyril of Alexandria: Festal Letters 13–30* (Washington, DC: Catholic University of America Press, 2013), 63.

of the Son of God; when the Lord was hungry or tried, Nestorius had to attribute that only to the son of Mary. Cyril saw that, if the Son of God was not hungry, tired, and finally crucified as a man – Mary's son – then the salvation of humanity was undone. He was not willing to divide Christ up on the basis of prefabricated definitions of 'divine' and 'human' and, instead, maintained a *unitive*, or a single-Son Christology which saw the Lord as truly God and truly human in one single acting subject. For Cyril, this was a non-negotiable of the incarnation, and the only way to see God and humanity united in salvation.

Anatomy of a Controversy

The controversy that followed was complex and a little background will help us, for Nestorius' theology did not mysteriously appear out of nowhere. His way of thinking about the person of Christ was the product of a cocktail of theological assumptions and philosophical commitments that we will explore over the next few chapters. His view of God, his telling of the story of salvation, and even his *definition* of salvation all connect to his Christology. Cyril – and much of the rest of the church of the day – could see how the puzzle fit together and attempted to offer a comprehensive rebuttal to the whole worrying picture. It was the Christology and the question of *Theotokos* that sparked the controversy, but the conflict went deceptively deep: it went to the very heart of the gospel and even the possibility of true fellowship between God and humanity. The picture of which this divisive Christology was one piece was a fundamentally un-Christian picture. And Nestorius did not paint it by himself.

Nestorius was born in Germanicia, Syria in around 386 and was trained in theology by Theodore of Mopsuestia (c.350–c.428), a long-serving bishop and noted biblical commentator. Theodore, in turn, had been mentored in the monastic life and theology by Diodore of Tarsus (d. 390).[27] Before becoming Bishop of Tarsus, Diodore had overseen a monastery in Antioch where he had taught both Theodore and John Chrysostom before him.[28] These three thinkers, Diodore, Theodore, and Nestorius are something of a dynasty and their theology is the main cause of the Christological controversy that erupted in the fifth century.[29] Nestorius was the man in the most public position and with the opportunity to influence the wider church, but it was essentially Diodore's and Theodore's theology that was finding its way into the mainstream through him.[30] Diodore had taught a Christology that became known as the 'Two Sons' Christology and Theodore had taught a related story of salvation that involved the man Jesus being helped to achieve moral perfection by a partnership with God the Word.[31] It is not hard to see why the Church, looking back at Diodore and Theodore at the second Council of Constantinople in 553, charged them with 'Nestorianism'. The label may have been retrofitted to a theological outlook that preceded Nestorius, but their theology was very much of a piece.[32]

Before we consider that theology – and Cyril's answers to it – it is worth seeking some clarity about the nature of the disagreement we are about to dive into. For a century and a half or so, popular level books on church history or early church theology have spoken about the disagreement between Cyril and Nestorius as symbolic of a clash between two great and venerable

27.   John Behr, *The Case Against Diodore and Theodore*, Oxford Early Christian Texts (Oxford: Oxford University Press, 2011), 48–59. See also Socrates, *Hist. Eccl.* 7.3.

28.   Socrates, *Hist. Eccl.* 6.3.

29.   See Norris, *Controversy*, 23–27.

30.   See Donald Fairbairn, *Grace and Christology in the Early Church* (Oxford: Oxford University Press, 2003), 28–29.

31.   See Fairbairn, *Grace and Christology*, 28–62; Behr, *Diodore and Theodore*, 28–34; Alois Grillmeier, *Christ in Christian Tradition: From the Apostolic Age to Chalcedon* (451). Trans. John Bowden. (London: Mowbray, 1975), 352–360.

32.   Fairbairn and Reeves, *Creeds and Confessions*, 48–108; Behr, *Diodore and Theodore*, 28–47, 83–100.

'schools' of theology with different Christological emphases, one in Antioch and the other in Alexandria. It is framed like the rivalry between Oxford and Cambridge or Harvard, Princeton, and Yale. It is as though great academics and churchmen from traditions of equal and opposite historical and spiritual dignity were represented in the Nestorian controversy. The Church, it is often imagined, was caught between these two great forces of nature, and could not quite make up its mind about which to prefer. The textbooks often tell the story that it was only at the Council of Chalcedon in 451 that the church managed to carve out a kind of compromise or halfway house that sought to honour the best of both the Antiochene and the Alexandrian perspectives or 'schools', especially when it came to Christology.[33]

The trouble is that historians and patristic specialists have been seriously questioning this old picture for decades. It simply does not fit the facts, nor the self-understanding of the theologians of the day.[34] It is true that, until the end of the fourth century, Alexandria was home to a catechetical school, according to a documented succession of its head teachers.[35] It is

33. See R. V. Sellers, *Two Ancient Christologies: A Study in the Christological Thought of the Schools of Antioch and Alexandria in the Early History of Christian Doctrine* (London: Society for Promoting Christian Knowledge, 1940); R. V. Sellers, *The Council of Chalcedon: A Historical and Doctrinal Survey* (London: Society for Promoting Christian Knowledge, 1953); G. W. H. Lampe and K. J. Woollcombe, *Essays on Typology, Studies in Biblical Theology* (Naperville, Ill: Alec R. Allenson, 1956); Justo González, *The Story of Christianity 1: The Early Church to the Dawn of the Reformation* (San Francisco: Harper & Row, 1984); Alister McGrath, *Historical Theology: An Introduction to the History of Christian Thought* (Hoboken, NJ: John Wiley and Sons, 2012).

34. See Donald Fairbairn, 'Patristic Exegesis and Theology: The Cart and the Horse', *Westminster Theological Journal* 69 (2007): 1–2; Frances Young, *Biblical Exegesis and the Formation of Christian Culture* (Cambridge: Cambridge University Press, 1997); John J. O'Keefe, '"A Letter that Killeth": Towards a Reassessment of Antiochene Exegesis, or Diodore, Theodore, and Theodoret on the Psalms', JECS 8, no. 1 (2000): 83–104.

35. See W. H. Oliver & M. J. S. Madise, 'The Formation of Christian Theology in Alexandria', *Verbum et Ecclesia* 35, no. 1 (2014); W. H. Oliver, 'The Heads of the Catechetical School in Alexandria', *Verbum et Ecclesia* 36, no. 1 (2015); and 'The

possible, too, that Antioch was the location of a monastic school of biblical exegesis, though this is disputed today.[36] But certainly neither city had a formal school of theology in operation by the time of Nestorian controversy in the fifth century.[37] The idea of two venerable academic institutions going head-to-head is impossible to hold, then. But what about two grand theological traditions? Are not Antioch and Alexandria the guardians of distinctive ways of reading Scripture, speaking about Jesus Christ, and organising theology which were (and are) equally useful to the Church?

Two Schools?

The old 'two schools' theory probably has its beginnings with John Henry Newman (1801–1890) who wanted to point out that Alexandria boasted a long line of notable scholars (such as Origen, Athanasius, and Cyril), many of whom devoted their lives to upholding theological orthodoxy. When Newman turned his eyes to Nestorius and friends in Antioch, he saw the city as Alexandria's 'evil twin' which was, to him, 'the very metropolis of heresy.'[38] But the account that has dominated the imagination of many for so long is undoubtedly that of the

---

Catechetical School in Alexandria', *Verbum et Ecclesia* 36, no. 1 (2015); N. Russell, *Cyril of Alexandria* (London: Routledge, 2000), 10.

36.   Paul Gavrilyuk, *The Suffering of the Impassable God*, Oxford Early Christian Studies (Oxford: Oxford University Press, 2004), 137; Richard J. Perhai, *Antiochene Theoria in the Writings of Theodore of Mopsuestia and Theodoret of Cyrus*, Emerging Scholars (Minneapolis: Fortress Press, 2015), 34.

37.   Gavrilyuk, *The Suffering of the Impassable God*, 137–138.

38.   Charles M. Stang, 'The Two "I"s of Christ: Revisiting the Christological Controversy', *Anglican Theological Review*, 94, no. 3 (2012): 532. Stang is quoting from Newman's *An Essay on the Development of Christian Doctrine*, second edition (James Toovey, 1846), 324. Newman also wrote that, 'it may almost be laid down as an historical fact that the mystical [i.e. Cyrillian] interpretation and orthodoxy will stand or fall together' (J. H. Newman. *The Arians of the Fourth Century* [Eugene: Wipf and Stock, 1996], 216). Newman, concerned as he was for the recovery of the theology of the early church fathers, clearly believed that the 'orthodox' tradition was under threat from the theology found in Antioch.

liberal Protestant church historian Adolf von Harnack (1851–1930). His *History of Dogma* sets out the 'two schools' paradigm perhaps most famously and influentially.

Harnack's portrait of the two brands of theology runs this way. The Antiochenes were marked by a methodical, historical, literalist reading of Scripture. Their philosophical outlook was dominated by the metaphysics of Aristotle. As a result of all this, they were likely to take very seriously the human life and experiences of Jesus – especially his free will as an independent man.[39] The Alexandrians, on the other hand, were driven by an allegorical reading of Scripture, paying more attention to possible spiritual or symbolic readings, and more closely aligned with Platonic philosophy. The result was a more mystical, divinely-focussed Christology which was constructed to uphold their framework of salvation.[40] This description from Harnack has gone deep into the bloodstream of the Church in the modern west to the point that it is almost ubiquitous. And, for many evangelicals, the so-called 'School of Antioch' look very much like the good guys. They are the ones who seem to take Scripture 'seriously' while the Alexandrians play fast and loose with allegory; they are the ones who believe in the true humanity of Jesus, while the Alexandrians are in danger of having him float three inches off the ground. At the very least, the so-called 'Antiochenes' are credited for 'emphasising' the humanity of Jesus while the Alexandrians so famously 'emphasised' his divinity. Many concede that Nestorius might have been pushing things too far – but so too, they say, could theologians from Alexandria. Take, for example Apollinarius, who had imagined Jesus possessing an incomplete humanity: the human soul replaced by the Word dwelling in its place.[41] Both 'schools', it is

---

39. Adolf von Harnack, *History of Dogma*, translated by W. M'Gilchrist, Theological Translation Library (London: Williams and Norgate, 1889–89), III: 155–6.

40. Harnack, *History of Dogma*, vol. III, 135; vol. II, 110.

41. See Stephen J. Wellum, *God the Son Incarnate: The Doctrine of Christ* (Wheaton: Crossway, 2016) 235ff. For a more provocative view, see Mark Edwards, *Catholicity*

said, had their extremists, but both had something constructive to contribute – perhaps even complimentary emphases. Perhaps the most responsible thing to do is try to balance the two and walk the tightrope between them. After all, that is what the Council of Chalcedon did in the end.

There are layers upon layers of assumptions here, like coats of paint that need to be stripped back one by one to reveal the original picture beneath. As these layers are removed, the familiar story of 'Alexandria versus Antioch' and of the church's ambivalence begins to dissolve.

It is most helpful to begin with the question of biblical interpretation. Increasingly, it is clear that many writers routinely described as 'Antiochene' do not necessarily employ wildly different methods of biblical exegesis to those classed as 'Alexandrian'.[42] So-called Antiochenes like John Chrysostom or Theodoret of Cyrus are capable of using allegory as much as any so-called Alexandrian, while the likes of Athanasius and Cyril are no less concerned with the historical or literary readings of the text than the former. Equally, thinkers meant to belong to the same 'school' very often come to very different conclusions in their interpretations.[43] There really is no hard

and Heresy in the Early Church (London, Routledge, 2009), 137–176.

42. See Fairbairn, 'Patristic Exegesis', 5–14; Frances M. Young, 'The Rhetorical Schools and Their Influence on Patristic Exegesis,' in The Making of Orthodoxy: Essays in Honour of Henry Chadwick Ed. Rowan Williams (Cambridge: Cambridge University Press, 1989); Alexander Kerrigan, St Cyril of Alexandria: Interpreter of the Old Testament (Rome: Pontificio Instituto Biblico, 1952).

43. See H. De Lubac, '"Typologie" et "allégorisme"', Recherches de science religieuse 34 (1947): 180–247; J. Guillet, 'Les Exégèsis d'Alexandrie et de Antioche: Conflict ou malentenddu?', Reserches de science religieuse 34 (1947): 257–302; Alexander Kerrigan, St Cyril of Alexandria: Interpreter of the Old Testament (Rome: Pontificio Instituto Biblico, 1952); F. Young, Biblical Exegesis and the Formation of Christian Culture (Cambridge: Cambridge University Press, 1997); Jaroslav Brož. 'From Allegory to the Four Senses of Scripture' in Philosophical Hermeneutics and Biblical Exegesis [Petr Pokorný, Jan Roskovec eds.] (Tübingen: Mohr Siebeck, 2002); Robert C. Hill (trans.), St Cyril of Alexandria: Commentary on the Twelve Prophets, vol. 1, Fathers of the Church 115 (Washington DC: Catholic University of America Press, 2007).

and fast 'Antiochene' or 'Alexandrian' way to read the Bible. The categories simply do not exist in that way. This means that imagining two ancient schools drawn into controversy by virtue of their conflicting Scriptural exegesis will not do as an explanation. Donald Fairbairn has argued persuasively that, given all this, the real point of conflict in the fifth century was *doctrinal*:

> Rather than asserting that exegesis was the horse pulling the theological cart, as the older view did, more recent scholarship has insisted that to a great degree, theology was the horse and exegesis the cart.[44]

Over the next chapters, as we consider the identity of Jesus Christ, the God He reveals, and the kind of salvation He offers, it will be clear that the church's soul-searching in the fifth century was about *theology* in its truest sense. It is in this realm that truly seismic differences emerge which go to the heart of the Christian faith. The fact that Cyril happens to have been an Alexandrian and that Nestorius and friends happen to have been from Antioch (or thereabouts) is not enough to understand the dynamics of their disagreement. It is certainly a mistake to imagine two great academic and spiritual powerhouses in a decades-long tug o' war for the church's seal of approval. The evidence suggests a different state of affairs altogether: Diodore, Theodore, and Nestorius stood as a relatively isolated trio with a very novel theological framework while Cyril gave voice to the great majority of the church in rejecting it, seeking simply to build upon the Council of Nicaea and Athanasius.[45]

---

44. Donald Fairbairn, 'Patristic Exegesis and Theology: The Cart and the Horse', *Westminster Theological Journal* 69 (2007): 10.

45. Cyril often signals his intention to carry on the work of those who had gone before him. See the Second and Third Letters to Nestorius which essentially act as commentaries on the Nicene Creed. He quotes Athanasius to support the use of *Theotokos* in his letter to the monks of Egypt (Letter 1). During the Council of Ephesus, after the reading of his second letter to Nestorius, Cyril said, 'I am confident that I shall be found to have departed in no way from the orthodox

We will trace the theology of Diodore, Theodore, and Nestorius – not as representatives of a great exegetical school but as theological outliers in their own time. In turn, we will trace the theology of the early church at large as expressed by Cyril and upheld in its councils as it sought to protect the truth about God, Christ, and salvation.

account of the faith or to have offended against the symbol issued by the holy and great council convened in its time at Nicaea, and I ask your sacredness to say whether this writing of mine is orthodox, unimpeachable, and in accord with that holy council or not.' Richard Price, trans., *The Council of Ephesus of 431: Documents and Proceedings*, TTH 72 (Liverpool: Liverpool University Press, 2020), 231–232. Cyril clearly saw himself – and positioned his argument – as Nicene. See also Metropolitan Serapion and Macarius Refela, 'St Cyril of Alexandria and the Council of Nicaea: The Framing of a Theological Controversy,' *The Ecumenical Review* 75, no. 2 (2003): 151–309.

3

JESUS: 'ONE LORD JESUS CHRIST'

Many of us have signed up for something on paper, with noble intentions and hearts in the right place, but then consistently undermined ourselves by our words and deeds. Our New Year's resolutions to diet or exercise are obvious and trivial examples; more serious are the marriage vows shattered by betrayal of trust or unfaithfulness. Just so, Diodore of Tarsus *intended* to be a staunch advocate of the Nicene orthodoxy, and he wanted to defend it from the errors of Arianism and Apollinarianism. We do not know much about Diodore, and what remains of his work comes to us in fragments, mostly quoted by other writers, but he is now best known for planting the seeds of Nestorianism with his so-called 'Two Sons' Christology. It is a tragic undoing of the very gospel truth he had hoped to protect.

When Diodore imagined the incarnate Christ, he did not want to deny his divinity like Arius did, neither did he want to compromise his true humanity as Apollinarius had. Seeing both true divinity and true humanity in one person, though, seemed to him very difficult – perhaps even inherently contradictory. Could it ever be right to speak about God *as* a human man and vice versa? What about the suffering and death of Jesus on the cross? Could that *really* be ascribed to God the Son? His solution was to regard the man Jesus and the Logos as *separate subjects* but refer to them both as 'Christ'. This way 'Christ' could be counted as both human and divine. Diodore was happy to speak about worshipping the man born of Mary, but *not* simply because he identified that man as God the Son. For Diodore, that could not strictly be true. He preferred to say that the man Jesus, son of Mary, had been 'assumed' by the eternal Word and could therefore be worshipped *along with Him*. They could now be considered together. He said,

> We adore the purple robes because of the one clothed, the temple because of the one indwelling, the form of the servant because of the form of God, the lamb because of the High Priest, the one assumed because of the one who assumed, the one who was formed in the womb of the virgin because of the creator of all.[1]

Jesus, he says, is due our worship *only because* He is caught up into a kind of relationship with God the Son. Even though there is one act of worship, seemingly offered to the one incarnate Christ, there are actually two recipients of it, side by side within and behind what is seen. One is the Creator, and one is created; One is the Emperor of the universe, the other is the kingly robe He wears; One is *truly* worthy of adoration, and the other included only by extension.

Theodore's Assumed Man

Diodore's protégé, Theodore of Mopsuestia, made a similar attempt to understand the incarnation and was also committed to the idea of Jesus as the 'assumed man'. Jesus, he said, was 'similar to all other men, differing from natural men in nothing

---

1.   Diodore is quoted here by Severus of Antioch in *Against the Impious Grammarian* 3.25 (possibly via Cyril), translated in John Behr, *The Case Against Diodore and Theodore*, Oxford Early Christian Texts (Oxford: Oxford University Press, 2011), 240-41.

except that he [the Logos] has given him grace'.[2] Just like Diodore, he did not think of Jesus *as* God the Son Himself, but as a man enjoying a unique relationship *with* the Son, especially characterised by grace. Even when Theodore tried to avoid talking about 'two sons' or 'two lords', he did so by 'first considering the God Word, he who by nature is Son of God, *then considering with him* the assumed, Jesus of Nazareth (...) who in the conjunction with the God Word partook of sonship and lordship...' and so was 'raised *together* to the title and honour of son and lord.'[3]

Jesus, the assumed man, comes to be included in, or to share in, what really only belonged to the *true* Son, as a separate person. Indeed, commenting on Hebrews 1:6, Theodore says that the assumed man had 'no [natural] communion with God the Word' but is made a 'partner' in his 'dignity'. He wonders,

> Who, therefore, is the one who is brought into the world and begins his mastery, requiring the angels to adore him? For someone would be mad to state that God the Word, who has given existence to everything... is the one who has been brought into the world.[4]

You would have to be mad, Theodore says, to believe that it was *actually* God the Word who was born in Bethlehem! Instead, Jesus is someone separate, 'a complete human being, the man born of Mary, who then freely cooperated with the Word in the work of salvation', as John Behr has summarised.[5] In fact, when, in John 12:30, Jesus hears the Father's voice from heaven and says, 'This voice has come for your sake, not mine', Theodore takes this to be a conversation between Jesus, the assumed man,

---

2. *De Incar.* 2, translated in Fairbairn, *Grace and Christology*, 42.

3. *The Exposition of the Faith*, quoted in *The Blasphemies of Diodore, Theodore, and the Impious Nestorius*, translated in Behr, *Diodore and Theodore*, 215 (emphasis mine).

4. *De Incar.* 12, in McLeod, *Theodore*, 139.

5. John Behr, *The Case Against Diodore and Theodore* (Oxford: Oxford University Press, 2011), 33.

and the Word.[6] Theodore sees the two as separate enough to hold conversation, to co-operate, and for the man to receive the grace of the Word.

Theodore thought that he had advanced on Diodore's understanding by using clearer terminology. He wanted to argue that there were two *physeis* ('natures' or 'concrete realities') in Christ (One the Word and the other, the assumed man), which were presented as a single *prosopon* ('manifest reality'). Even the most charitable reader would have to confess that it seemed like Theodore's Christ was a thin veil over two separate personal subjects who had agreed to co-operate for a time.[7] As the Nestorian controversy began to simmer, Cyril was carefully reading Theodore's work and collecting ammunition for later, knowing it to be the source of Nestorius' thought.[8]

Nestorius and the Glass Wall

When Nestorius came to prominence, it was really Theodore's Christology that he popularised and he, too, would speak about the two *physeis* combined in Christ's one *prosopon*. In his first sermon against the use of *Theotokos* in 428, he said quite plainly that he saw the Lord as 'twofold'.[9] He was very clear that, while there is only one Christ available to human view, behind the scenes, the man and the Word are invisibly but very definitely partitioned off from one another. This is known as his theory of 'prosopic union'.

---

6. Behr, *Diodore and Theodore*, 33.

7. For guidance on the exact meanings at various points of the terms *ousia, physis, hypostasis*, and *prosopon*, see John McGuckin's *The Christological Controversy*, 138–51, and the excellent table and explanation in Donald Fairbairn and Ryan Reeves' *The Story of Creeds and Confessions*, 86–88.

8. See Behr, *Diodore and Theodore*, 88; 133–159. Behr shows that Cyril is carefully dealing with the writings of Diodore and Theodore as early as 428. See also McGuckin, *The Christological Controversy*, 32.

9. Nestorius, 'Nestorius's First Sermon against the *Theotokos*' quoted in Norris, *The Christological Controversy*, 129.

When Nestorius opened the Gospels and saw Jesus admitting very human limitations in his knowledge, or being tired and hungry, he said that these things could only be associated with the *physis* of the man. The Word surely remained untouched by such lowly, creaturely concerns. Meanwhile, when Christ claimed divine authority or performed miraculous signs, this was clearly the *physis* of the Word at work, and the human being was kept safe from eclipse or obliteration by the greater power.[10] As we will see in the next chapter, Nestorius was especially concerned to restrict the suffering of the cross to the man Jesus and distance the Word from it at all costs. Each *physis* is sealed off from the identity and experiences of the other.

Nestorius was able to speak of the man and the Word in this way, coming to the fore at different moments during the life of Christ because, he said, they had a relationship of 'conjunction' (*synapheia*). And 'relationship' is the right word, for Nestorius believed each to be separate enough to exist in a kind of mutually agreed partnership. Their co-operation is grounded in the gracious will of God to assume the man, and the man reciprocated 'morally', righteously choosing what God willed for him. In his later work, *The Book of Heracleides*, Nestorius speaks of the two as 'united by love', so jointly committed to their conjunction that, for anyone to look upon the incarnate Christ is to see a perfect union of the two.[11] Echoing Theodore, he said,

> I revere the one who is borne because of the one who carries him, and I worship the one I see because of the one who is hidden… I divide the natures, but unite the worship.[12]

It is technically possible to describe all this as 'Christ in two natures' since the terminology can easily be taken this way on

---

10. E.g. Sermon 10 in F. Loofs, *Nestoriana* (Halle: M. Niemeyer, 1905), 275.

11. Nestorius, *The Book of Heracleides* 1.1.58, in G. R. Driver and L. Hodgson (eds.) *Nestorius: The Bazaar of Heracleides* (Oxford: Clarendon Press, 1925), 55.

12. Nestorius, 'First Sermon' in *The Book of Heracleides*, 130.

face value. But our familiarity with that slightly ambivalent phrase would rather obscure what Nestorius was teaching. He may have been saying *that* there are two *physeies* or 'natures' in Christ, but he was dangerously unclear about *who* this Christ is. On the one hand, the Word seems to be present and acting on earth in the incarnation, but a glass wall runs almost invisibly down the middle of Christ dividing Him from the man Jesus, who is, after all, the one who was born of Mary, lived, died, and was raised to life for our salvation. As Stephen Holmes remarks, 'all that is ontologically significant for Nestorius remains *two*'.[13] The one 'Christ' is only a *prosopon* – little more than a cipher or conceptual tool for the united presentation of the two.

What would it mean for our knowledge of God and our salvation if Jesus and the Word were not identical? In other words, if Jesus were not the exact same *person* as the one who is eternally one with the Father? Nestorius seems to answer that the man Jesus is the source of our salvation *through his union with the Word*. As Jesus obediently lived in relationship with the Word, he was given grace to submit himself even to death and then be raised from the tomb. This unique enabling grace on the man Jesus, means that he becomes a trailblazer for our salvation as we follow him. Instead of being a Saviour stepping down from heaven to rescue sinners, this is a champion raised up from among us as an example to be followed.

Cyril could see that Nestorius' Jesus was only a man like the rest of us, elevated to a special relationship with God. The one who suffered and died on the cross was not strictly *God the Son Himself* coming to us in the flesh. Instead, God placed the man Jesus between Himself and sinful humanity, as though to keep His hands clean as He dealt with us. Rather than embracing us directly, He assumed a man into prosopic union, promoted him to divine dignity, and set him before us as a supercharged

---

13. Stephen R. Holmes 'Reformed Varieties of the *Communicatio Idiomatum*' in Stephen R. Holmes and Murray A. Rae (eds.) *The Person of Christ* (Edinburgh: T & T Clark, 2005), 83 (my emphasis).

example of holiness to imitate. Cyril knew that this Jesus could not be the Saviour spoken of in the Scriptures. We will explore these things in the next two chapters.

But first, how did Cyril speak of Jesus Christ?

One Lord Jesus Christ

The baseline for Cyril is that the man Jesus is none other than God the Son come down from heaven to save humanity. Nestorius and his friends imagined two sons, but Cyril saw only one. While Nestorius' Jesus made an *upward* journey, co-operating with the Son of God, aided by grace, and attaining resurrection, Cyril's Jesus was none other than the Son of God Himself: the Son on a *downward* journey, stepping into the world in grace and love. This is really nothing more than the logic of Philippians 2:5-6. Here, Paul applies the name 'Christ Jesus' to the eternal Son as he describes Him considering and then choosing the path of incarnation, humility, servanthood, and crucifixion. Someone may object that the human baby named 'Jesus' had not yet been born in Bethlehem when the Son made this decision, but Paul is clearly content to use the name retrospectively. It presents no problem to him, since he has in mind the same single person at all points in the narrative. The divine One who humbled Himself *is* Jesus of Nazareth: a *single* Son, perfect in His deity and humanity, for

> the Son humbled himself because of love... that he became man for us and did not fall out of his divinity but remains the I AM.[14]

Cyril's second and third letters to Nestorius are important sources for his presentation of this Christology. The second letter explained that his view of Christ is taken directly from the Nicene Creed:

---

14. Cyril, *Commentary on Hebrews*, 39.

The holy and great council said that the only begotten Son himself, begotten of God the Father according to his nature, true God of true God, light of light, he through whom the Father made all things, descended, was made flesh and became man, suffered, rose on the third day and ascended into heaven. We must follow these words and teachings, keeping in mind what having been made flesh means; and that it makes clear that the Logos from God became man.[15]

Cyril wants to be very clear that the Word did not change from One (divine) thing into another (human) thing, but that He united to Himself a true and whole human nature. The two natures are not somehow blended into one new thing because they are clearly distinct. But neither are the two separate personalities in co-operation, as Nestorius had said. Cyril writes:

We do not say that the nature of the Word was altered when he became flesh. Neither do we say that the Word was changed into a complete man of soul and body. We say rather that the Word by having united to himself hypostatically flesh animated by a rational soul, inexplicably and incomprehensibly became man. He has been called the Son of man, not according to desire alone or goodwill, nor by the assumption of a person only. We say that, although the natures are different which were brought together to a true unity, there is one Christ and Son from both. The differences of the natures are not destroyed through the union, but rather the divinity and humanity formed for us one Lord Jesus Christ and one Son through the incomprehensible and ineffable combination to a unity.[16]

Because of this, Cyril chose to use very different language to that of Nestorius. Nestorius had seen Jesus and the Word conjoined into one *prosopon* by their love for one another. Cyril preferred to say that the Word *hypostatically* or 'personally' joined Himself

15. Cyril's Second Letter to Nestorius Letter 4 in McEnerney, *St Cyril of Alexandria: Letters 1–50*, 39.

16. Cyril's Second Letter to Nestorius, Letter 4 in McEnerney, *St Cyril of Alexandria: Letters 1–50*, 39.

to human flesh.[17] Because of that union, the human man who was born in Bethlehem and died in Jerusalem was precisely the Word *in flesh*. God the Son is the one person active in the incarnation. In the early days of these discussions, especially, Cyril would speak of only 'one incarnate *physis* of God the Word', meaning one incarnate 'person' or Son.[18] He does not speak about any mutual 'will' or 'pleasure' or 'love' *between* the divine and the human, because he does not see the man Jesus as a *separate person* to act or love in response to the Word. Instead, when the man Jesus does come to act and love, it is God the Son doing all these things *as a human man*. To put it another way, the human flesh was *hypostasised* or 'made personal' by the Word as was not a person without him. This is what has become known as the doctrine of the hypostatic union. The Word *personally* took humanity to Himself so that it was really and truly His own. Unlike Diodore, Theodore, and Nestorius, Cyril did not see the humanity of Christ as a different personal subject, but one Christ, Son, and Lord: divine *and* human.

The Economy of his Flesh

When Cyril writes about this union of divine and human in Christ, he has a very clear focus on what he calls the *oikonomia* ('economy') of the incarnation.[19] He is aware that it would be easy to get caught up in a philosophical tug o' war with Nestorius about what *should* and should *not* be technically possible for divine and human natures or how to use the word *physis*, but he

---

17. Cyril's Second and Third Letters to Nestorius are crucial sources for this terminology in his writing.

18. See especially Cyril's second letter to Succensus, Letter 46 in McEnerney, St Cyril of Alexandria: Letters 1-50, 198-204. See Fairbairn, *Grace and Christology*, 126-129 for a survey of Cyril's use of this term. Fairbairn makes a clear argument that Cyril is not imagining a single *new* nature concocted from the divine and human, but one Son who is both truly divine and truly human. See also Hans van Loon, *The Dyophysite Christology of Cyril of Alexandria* (Leiden: Brill, 2009), 531-543.

19. Examples include *St. Luke*, vol. 1, serm. 11, 47, 53; *Scholia* 5 (ACO 1.5, 184-231); *On the Unity of Christ 118*; *Second Letter to Succensus 2*, and many more.

wants to begin with the fact that the Word really *did* join Himself to humanity and really *did* all that is recorded in the Gospels *as a man*. This is his starting point: the 'ineffable' and 'inexpressible' reality that God the Son personally came to do all this. Why? How? – *For us* and for our salvation!

John McGuckin puts it this way:

> [t]o say that the Logos was born is, for Cyril, not the nonsense Nestorius thought it to be, any more than to say the Logos suffered or died, because the apparent paradox brings home to the believer the constantly presumed context – that these things, birth, suffering, death, and resurrection, took place "economically", that is as a practical exercise of the Logos who assumed a human bodily life not pointlessly but in order to work out the salvation of the human race in its bodily condition; first in the divine transformation of his own authentically human life, and then (as he was the paradigm of salvation in his resurrection) in the transformation of christians.[20]

The logic of the concept is captured – although the word is not used directly – in Cyril's third letter to Nestorius when Cyril writes,

> He had no natural need, or external necessity, of a temporal birth in these last times of this age, but he did this so that he might bless the very beginning of our own coming into being, and that since a woman had given birth to him as united to the flesh, from that point onwards, the curse upon our whole race should cease that drives our earthly bodies to death.[21]

In other words, the actions of the incarnate Son are more than isolated phenomena which invite intense theological speculation, but are true and real actions of *God the Son in His flesh*. They were planned and enacted for the purpose of our true and real salvation and cannot be understood or appreciated outside of it. The concept of the 'economy' is really a way to say that Scripture

20. McGuckin, *The Christological Controversy*, 184.

21. *Second Letter to Nestorius* 11, in McGuckin, *The Christological Controversy*, 273.

and the Nicene Creed require a kind of *soteriological* Christology – a way of understanding the person of Christ that is driven by His *actual* coming to save us. Finessing Christological language and adopting abstract concepts alone cannot get to the root of what God has *actually done* in Christ.

The Communication of Idioms

Since Cyril is committed to thinking about the one Son of God in this way, he is happy to speak of the actions of Christ in the incarnation in a truly united way, whether divine or human. He can speak about the actions of the Word in His eternal divine nature (continuing to fill the universe and sustain it) and the actions of the Word in His new human nature ('sharing blood and body... found like us in everything')[22] – and say both things in the same breath about *the same person*. This is the principle of the communication of idioms. As Thomas Weinandy has it, 'all those attributes that pertain to his divinity or humanity are predicated of one and the same Son.'[23]

In the economy of the incarnation, for the first and last time, both divine and human characteristics and actions can rightly be attributed to one person. Both obviously human *and* obviously divine attributes now belong to Jesus Christ in a unified way.[24] We see this in Scripture where one touch from Jesus' *human* hand raises a dead girl (Mark 5:41), and in Acts 20:28, the church is bought with *God's* own blood. God does not have blood to shed and human hands cannot heal – except in the divine-human

---

22. *Commentary on Hebrews*, 255–265.

23. Thomas Weinandy and Daniel A. Keating, *The Theology of St Cyril of Alexandria* (Edinburgh: T&T Clark, 2003), 28.

24. Andrew McGinnis points out that, in Letters 39 and 41 especially, Cyril sees Christ's 'from-above-ness' as a continual personal property that is not relinquished in the incarnation but expressed in it. 'The Son adds to himself human nature and all its physicality, infirmities, and sufferings (sin excepted), but the Son's personal heavenliness and transcendence endures'. Andrew M. McGinnis, *The Son of God Beyond the Flesh: A Historical and Theological Study of the Extra Calvinisticum* (London: Bloomsbury, 2014), 27.

person Jesus Christ. This is hypostatic union being worked out in the real-life conditions of the economy of the incarnation. The humanity of the Son *really is His own* and, because of the union, *is Him*. This principle means that, as R. L. Ottley says, 'the Logos can be said to suffer, hunger, thirst, learn, pray; while, on the other hand, the manhood can be adored, and the body called "divine".'[25]

It was the communication of idioms that allowed believers to express in simple language the stunning and mind-bending humility of the Son. As we saw in the last chapter, Christians were fond of speaking of 'God wrapped in swaddling bands' at Christmas and 'God the Word who died on the cross' at Easter.[26] While Nestorius rejected these turns of phrase along with *Theotokos*, Cyril felt they were the natural result of a non-negotiable doctrinal move.[27] The person in view from manger to cross to ascension was the Word in flesh, and any sense of contradiction or tension in this was to be embraced.[28]

For Cyril, this does not mean that humanity and divinity are somehow blended or mixed together in Jesus. They do not lose their distinctness or meld into a third new thing but are 'ineffably and inexplicably united'.[29] Cyril did not intend that anything improper should be ascribed to either nature: *Theotokos* no more means that the Word first came into being through Mary than 1 Corinthians 5:17 means that the human cells, organs, and face of Jesus existed eternally and came down from heaven. Nevertheless, the great shock of the economy of the incarnation was precisely that *the Word* became a helpless

---

25. R. L. Ottley, *The Doctrine of the Incarnation* (London: Methuen & Co, 1946), 404.

26. McGuckin, *The Christological Controversy*, 151–152.

27. See, for example, Cyril's Festal Letter 17, written in 429 (Amidon and O'Keefe, *Festal Letters 13–30*, 66): 'the divine, transcendent infant, just born, was in swaddling clothes.'

28. Cf. Cyril's *Third Letter to Nestorius* 6, 8. We will look at more examples of this in the next chapter.

29. Letter 46 in McEnerney, *St Cyril of Alexandria: Letters 1–50*, 200–201.

baby, suffered, died, and was resurrected for us. When Jesus was tempted and emerged victorious (Matt 4:1), suffered and so learned obedience (Heb 5:8), and endured the cross, submitting His will to the Father (Matt 26:42), this was truly the Word being tempted, learning, and submitting *in His newly taken humanity.* We might say that, at every moment of His earthly life, the Son was 'true to Himself' as the Father's holy, perfect, and beloved Son. Through each trial and sorrow He faced, he faithfully and beautifully embodied and revealed the life of God. Jesus was God, but now in the conditions of a real, emotional, difficult human life, right from His conception to His ascension into heaven.

Nestorius believed that when Cyril assigned divine and human experience to the same person, he was revealing himself to be Apollinarian.[30] Cyril resisted this charge since, while Nestorius thought the idea of the Word dying on the cross was theologically inaccurate, Cyril saw that it was the whole point of the economy.[31] The eternal Word Himself was personally the subject of all the acts of the incarnation. God the Son Himself knew tiredness, temptation, and death in His flesh for the sake of human salvation. He did not join Himself to a separate human person with which to shield His deity from these things. Nestorius later protested that Cyril 'has attributed nothing in the Incarnation to the conduct of the man but [all] to God the Word'.[32] Cyril might well have responded: there is nobody else *but* God the Word! It was all Him.

Ephesus: The End of the Matter?

Cyril's third letter to Nestorius in 430 had included twelve 'anathemas' – a series of theological ultimatums that, he believed,

---

30. See his reply to Cyril's Second Letter, 7 in McGuckin, *The Christological Controversy*, 367.

31. Cyril is not arguing for Theopaschitism, here (the belief that God can suffer) any more than Apollinarianism. See chapter four for a discussion of this in more detail.

32. Nestorius, *Heracleides* 1.2, 91.

Nestorius surely could not ignore.[33] To be pronounced anathema is to be cursed and cut off as a heretic, and Cyril clearly hoped that twelve shots across Nestorius' bough would stun him into sense. As the stakes rose, so the conflict intensified through the year, and both men hoped for key figures in the church to take their side. Each had been in correspondence with Celestine, Bishop of Rome, hoping for backup; each suspected Emperor Theodosius to be on his side and soon to pronounce against the other.

In the end, Theodosius called an ecumenical council at Pentecost in June of 431 with a mandate to investigate the Christological controversy. The church's third such council (after Nicaea in 325 and Constantinople in 381) was to be held in Ephesus.[34] The city, once dedicated to the goddess Artemis, had unofficially transferred its affection to Mary the Mother of God, and Nestorius will have squirmed upon hearing the news: it was not a good sign for him. To make it worse from his perspective, it was clear that Celestine, along with most of the western bishops, was coming down firmly on Cyril's side. Perhaps worst of all for Nestorius, Cyril was chosen as the council's president.

Ephesus was a powder keg that summer. From the moment of his arrival in the city, Nestorius thoroughly resented being there and tried to hamper proceedings, ignoring three separate summons to appear before the council. He directed much of his frustration at Cyril, whom he regarded as a troublemaker and self-promoter. But his irritation only grew and broadened as the start of the council was significantly delayed. Sixteen delegates arrived over a week late, while several eastern bishops made Nestorius wait even longer. It will have hurt him that these were his countrymen and allies, led by his old friend, John of

---

33. Letter 17 in McEnerney, *St Cyril of Alexandria: Letters 1–50*, 80–92.

34. For the records and associated documents, see Richard Price, trans., *The Council of Ephesus of 431: Documents and Proceedings*, TTH 72 (Liverpool: Liverpool University Press, 2020). Also useful is Donald Fairbairn and Ryan Reeves, *The Story of Creeds and Confessions*.

Antioch, whom he expected might speak in support of him. Their lateness was partly down to an arduous journey by camel from Syria involving flooding, unexpected detours, beasts of burden giving out, and fatal illness, but probably also betrayed a similar recalcitrance to that of Nestorius himself. As the waiting weeks passed and the days grew warmer, the air crackled with tension. Both Cyril and Nestorius (and various sub-groups of their supporters) had arrived in town with armed guards and there were reports of bishops physically fighting one another, intimidation, and vandalism of buildings. Nestorius, writing later in his life about that time, complained that

> the followers [of Cyril] ... went about in the city girt and armed with clubs... with the yells of barbarians, snorting fiercely... carrying bells about the city and lighting fires... They blocked up the streets so that everyone was obliged to flee and hide, while they acted as masters of the situation, lying about, drunk and besotted and shouting obscenities.[35]

It is very unlikely that Cyril and his companions had much to do with any disturbances and unrest – he certainly denied such rumours explicitly – but he was no less provocative in writing home that Nestorius, 'the wretch, that sleepless beast, goes about' devilishly 'plotting against the glory of Christ' but that 'his wickedness gains nothing.'[36] At least one of Nestorius' supporters deserted him in disgust after an argument in which Nestorius treated him as though he were stupid, spluttering, 'We must not call the one who became man for us, God' and 'I refuse to acknowledge as God, an infant of two or three months old.'[37] Sixty or so bishops who had arrived as 'floating voters' were soon choosing Cyril's side. This meant that, for some weeks, one of Nestorius' only real friends in Ephesus was the emperor's

35.   Nestorius, *Heracleides* 2.1.

36.   Cyril, Letter 21 in McEnerney, *St Cyril of Alexandria: Letters 1–50*, 100.

37.   McGuckin, *The Christological Controversy*, 64.

representative, Candidian.[38] He had been entrusted by the emperor (who had remained in Constantinople) with keeping peace and maintaining order at the gathering, but he clashed several times with Cyril and his supporters who wanted to move quickly and have the council over and done with. Candidian, seemingly enjoying the exercise of his authority, was determined to wait for the arrival of John.

Nevertheless, two weeks after it had been due to begin, Cyril unilaterally opened the Council of Ephesus in the Church of St. Mary on Monday 22nd June. As nearly 200 bishops began to gather and take their seats, Candidian burst into the church and demanded that proceedings cease and everyone go to their rooms.[39] The session could only begin, he said, once he had personally read the imperial declaration to formally initiate proceedings. Until then, he huffed, their gathering was technically illegal. The bishops were not best pleased to be slapped on the wrist like naughty children; much less to be told that they – a group of senior clergymen – were not being allowed to gather in a church. Sensing his moment, Cyril innocently asked Candidian what this very important declaration said. As McGuckin wonderfully puts it, 'in the sublime confidence of his annoyance Candidian proceeded to read it.'[40] The council had begun.

It seems that Nestorius and Cyril did not meet in person at all during their time in the same town. Nestorius and his friends refused to attend and soldiers with clubs sent away the messengers who summoned him. He protested the absence of John of Antioch and others, but Cyril pointed out that other bishops who had travelled further than John had made it in good time. John had apparently sent word that the council should get going without him anyway. The Christologies of

38.   Price, *The Council of Ephesus*, 48.

39.   Price, *The Council of Ephesus*, 48; 217–291; 305ff.

40.   McGuckin, *The Christological Controversy*, 78.

Cyril and Nestorius were sampled, discussed, and compared with earlier theological works. It took only a day to establish that the attendees were content to acclaim (that is, formally adopt) Cyril's second letter to Nestorius. The gathered bishops regarded it as a solid statement of Christological orthodoxy and felt that Cyril's critique of Nestorius was accurate and just. The bishops were generally dismayed that Nestorius seemed to think he alone properly understood the truth of the incarnation. They heard that Nestorius had blamed them for what he said was the 'ignorance' of the laity: 'your teachers have not had the occasion to present the doctrines to you in a properly exact fashion.' [41] Bishop Capreolus of Carthage had written to the council begging the bishops not to tolerate any innovation in the faith and, when his letter was read, those present agreed that Nestorius was doing just such a thing.[42] On the reading of excerpts from Nestorius' sermons and writings, the bishops condemned Nestorius (who had still not bothered to show his face) as 'the new Judas' and deposed him, removing him from his ministry with immediate effect.[43] Cyril's letter home that day claimed that virtually the whole of Ephesus turned out, waiting from dawn to dusk to hear the outcome of the council. The fall of Nestorius, an 'enemy of the faith', apparently so delighted the crowds that they paraded the bishops to a local tavern by torchlight, singing and calling out praise to God as they went.[44]

Yet the council was far from over. While the bishops gleefully toasted their efficiency and concord, Nestorius was writing a

---

41. These details can be found in ACO 1.2.45–64, translated in McGuckin, *The Christological Controversy*, 369–378; see also Price, *The Council of Ephesus*, 277.

42. Price, *The Council of Ephesus*, 279.

43. Price, *The Council of Ephesus*, 299.

44. Cyril, Letter 24. This is a satisfyingly poetic moment since Athanasius had once complained that Alexandria's taverns had been the venue for the singing of Arian songs. These patrons clearly had a different song. See Hass, *Alexandria in Late Antiquity*, 68, and Carlos R. Galvão-Sobrinho, *Doctrine and Power: Theological Controversy and Christian Leadership in the Later Roman Empire* (Berkeley: University of California Press, 2013), 51–65.

grievance to the emperor.[45] He had not been treated fairly, he said, and wanted a rerun of the council. On receiving the letter, along with one from Cyril (who assumed all that remained to do was some paperwork), Theodosius seemingly threw up his hands, sick of it all: Cyril, Nestorius, and the useless Candidian, whose own account he received later, too. Before he could find any resolution, however, John arrived in Ephesus at long last, now three weeks late, on 26th June. On hearing of Nestorius' experience and the way Cyril had led proceedings, John assembled a spontaneous (and imperially unsanctioned) 'mini council' of 43 bishops. They declared Cyril to be an Apollinarian heretic and therefore excommunicated.[46] The emperor, overwhelmed with the clergy of Constantinople lobbying him daily, forbade any bishop to leave Ephesus and wrote that no decision from either the large or small council would stand unless he permitted it.[47] The city was in uproar and things became increasingly chaotic. John seems to have arranged for signs to be made denouncing the original council as Apollinarian. Cyril and his friend, Memnon, Bishop of Ephesus, challenged John's council and declared *him* excommunicated.[48] Cyril was placed under house arrest and forced to send letters secretly, one smuggled out of the city concealed in the hollowed-out staff of a man disguised as an old beggar.[49] Elderly bishops began to die in the heat.[50] The emperor temporarily upheld the decisions of *both* councils, holding Nestorius, John, Cyril, and Memnon all to be deposed.

---

45. Nestorius accuses the Egyptians and Asians of 'sending out the rabble-rousers' and rioters into the market square to 'fill the city with confusion.' Price, *The Council of Ephesus*, 309–312.

46. Price, *The Council of Ephesus*, 324–331.

47. Price, *The Council of Ephesus*, 356–358.

48. Price, *The Council of Ephesus*, 400.

49. McGuckin, *The Christological Controversy*, 80–84; Price, *The Council of Ephesus*, 312–315.

50. McGuckin, *The Christological Controversy*, 102.

All this rumbled on through to the autumn before the various sessions were finished.

The council had been farcical in many ways. Richard Price writes that since no doctrinal definitions were agreed, there is no sense of a formal solution to the questions that had been debated.[51] Yet, there was a kind of *de facto* conclusion. Theodosius eventually came to the realisation that the bishops at the original council far outnumbered those who supported Nestorius, and some were still leaving his side to join the majority.[52] The emperor essentially accepted the outcome of the original council and restored Cyril to his ministry, but Nestorius' condemnation was to stand.[53] After nearly two months of chaos and confusion, Cyril and his theology had won out and he left Ephesus in mid-October, when the council was formally closed by the emperor.[54] The Council of Ephesus had endorsed the title *Theotokos*, upheld Cyril's understanding of the hypostatic union of the natures rather than a 'conjunction' and rejected 'two sons' Christology. The teaching of Nestorius was judged unacceptable and marginal. Even John of Antioch now distanced himself from his old friend, Nestorius, and his theology.[55]

After Ephesus

The Council of Ephesus understandably leaves many historians (and theologians) with a bad taste in their mouths. Its outcome was decisive, but the process was a mess; the theological implications are clear, but the aftermath was complex. Theological questions and tensions lingered that would require another council, that of Chalcedon in 451. It is here, too, that the caricature of

---

51. Price, *The Council of Ephesus*, 83–84.

52. McGuckin, *The Christological Controversy*, 106.

53. McGuckin, *The Christological Controversy*, 106; Price, *The Council of Ephesus*, 589–590.

54. McGuckin, *The Christological Controversy*, 107; Price, *The Council of Ephesus*, 587–590.

55. McGuckin, *The Christological Controversy*, 102.

Cyril 'the bully' tends to pop up in popular literature. Some writers imagine Cyril marching around Ephesus with his 600 *parabalani* (which he did not; they were stationed nearly a thousand miles away in Egypt), while poor Nestorius cowered in his quarters.[56] Some historians suggest that Cyril bribed his way back into office, citing his Letter 96 which details an incredible shipment of treasure from Alexandria to the imperial court at Constantinople.[57] The docket lists piles of gold, woollen rugs, ivory chairs, cauldrons, and eight ostriches (which may or may not be pieces of furniture). There is no doubt that some underhand business went on here. The court of Theodosius was notoriously corrupt, and a reference to 'customary suppliant gifts' in the paperwork suggests this was clearly the established way of getting things done in Constantinople.[58] These payments to various officials did not buy Cyril's reinstatement or the verdict of the council, but likely ensured a more favourable and prompt resolution after endless prevarication on the emperor's part. It seems he arrived home in Alexandria on 31st October.[59]

Nestorius, meanwhile, was sent back to his monastery in Antioch. Eventually, he was exiled variously in Petra, the Holy Land, and several locations in Egypt, during which it seems he endured quite a traumatic time.[60] One ancient tradition relates him surviving an assassination attempt by Alexandrian monks. Another tells the story of him being kidnapped along with some companions, and the whole group (including the kidnappers) nearly dying of thirst in the desert. Nestorius miraculously

---

56. McGuckin, *The Christological Controversy*, 80.

57. See Zoran Đurović, 'Bribe of St. Cyril of Alexandria', *Theological Views* XLVI, no. 2 (2013): 395-406; Maurits Sterk de Leeuw, 'Buying Imperial Favour: Cyril of Alexandria's Blessings' in Kamil Cyprian Choda, Maurits Sterk de Leeuw, and Fabian Schulz, *Gaining and Losing Imperial Favour in Late Antiquity* (Leiden: Brill, 2019), 150-170.

58. Cyril, Letter 96, in John I. McEnerney, *St Cyril of Alexandria: Letters 51-110*, Fathers of the Church 77 (Catholic University of American Press, repr. 2007), 151-153.

59. Price, *The Council of Ephesus*, 587, 590.

60. McGuckin, *The Christological Controversy*, 117-118.

opened a spring in the desert, saving the lives of all present, so that the criminals set their hostages free in gratitude. The same source claims that Nestorius received prophetic knowledge of Cyril's death while in prayer, long before the news was circulated. Less friendly sources claimed that he died through the rotting of his limbs and tongue, or that he was struck down by an angel one day while loudly blaspheming the Mother of God as he relieved himself. His intestines apparently exploded and, when his absence was noted the next day and his door forced open, his remains were found in the toilet.[61]

It is hard to believe that any of these traditions are especially reliable! We do know that the last of Nestorius' exiles was in remote Panopolis (today's Akhmim), just beside the Nile, in Cyril's own diocese.[62] It was here, likely in 451 or 452, that he wrote the *Book of Heracleides* – one of the only texts of his which survives in full – and which reflects on his life and restates his theology. It is sometimes said that it reveals a more sympathetic figure, presenting a Christology nowhere near as problematic as Cyril and others had feared. This is a puzzling conclusion! *The Book of Heracleides* is just as clear as any of Nestorius' earlier writings about his divisive Christology. He complains about the bishops who formed the Council of Ephesus ('O wise judges' he writes, positively dripping with sarcasm),[63] and accuses Cyril of insincerity, claiming he had deliberately misrepresented him to the council, fuddling them with 'definitions, with furious words, as robbers' to hide his true purpose (though it is unclear what this purpose might have been).[64] The 17 bishops who had supported Nestorius to the end were removed from their sees, and Nestorianism was soon a byword for heresy.

---

61. See Rafał Kosiński, The Life of Nestorius as seen in Greek and Oriental Sources, *Electrum* 13 (2007): 155-170.

62. Kosiński, *The Life of Nestorius*, 155-170.

63. Nestorius, *Heracleides* 2.1, 170.

64. Nestorius, *Heracleides* 2.1, 161.

Happily, two years after the Council of Ephesus, in 433, Cyril and John of Antioch came to a brotherly understanding. Having kept up correspondence after the condemnation of Nestorius, they agreed on a statement of Christology known as 'The Formula of Reunion'.

> We confess that our Lord Jesus Christ, the only begotten Son of God, is perfect God and perfect man, of a rational soul and body, begotten before ages from the Father according to his divinity, and that, in recent days, he himself for us and for our salvation was born from the Virgin Mary according to his humanity, consubstantial to the Father himself according to divinity and consubstantial to us according to his humanity, for a union was made of his two natures. We confess one Christ, one Son, one Lord. With this understanding of a union without fusion we confess that the Holy Virgin is the Mother of God, because God the Word was made flesh and was made man, and from his very conception he united to himself a temple taken from her. And we know that theologians regard some of the evangelical and apostolic sayings regarding the Lord as common, that is, as pertaining to one person, and that theologians divide others of the sayings as pertaining to two natures, and refer those proper to God to the divinity of Christ, but the lowly ones to his humanity.[65]

It was an admirable exercise in mutual understanding and co-operation on the part of both men, showing John's openness to changing his mind and Cyril's willingness to moderate the strong language of his 12 anathemas. With appropriate caveats and expressions of humility, they agreed on the sufficiency of the Nicene Creed for settling Christological discussions, the correctness of the *Theotokos* title, and a union of two natures in one person. They also agreed to allow some latitude in theological language. Specifically on Cyril's part, he accepted that people were using the word *physis* with different intentions.

---

65.   Cyril, Letter 39 in McEnerney, *Letters 1–50*, 148–149.

Cyril himself had frequently used the catchphrase 'one incarnate *physis* of God the Logos' to refer to one *person* or Son in the incarnation, while Nestorius had used *physis* to speak of two *persons*. Still others were using it to refer to the two *natures* in the one person of the Son, or the natural properties of those natures – even Cyril himself did this on occasion.[66] Without budging on his central critique of Nestorianism, that there could only be *one person* (note this language in the formula, which would go on to shape the Chalcedonian Definition later), Cyril conceded that this use of *physis* was orthodox – although it had not consistently been his preference. Both men had to bear the cost of their reconciliation: John's Nestorian-leaning friends thought he had capitulated to Apollinarianism, and some of Cyril's more inflexible followers were equally disappointed in the opposite direction. Nevertheless, Cyril was able to write to John, 'my beloved brother and fellow bishop' that 'every manner of disagreement has been removed'.[67]

Cyril maintained that his convictions had remained unchanged, he had ceded no ground to Nestorianism, and cleared himself of any charge of Apollinarianism. The Bishop of Rome wrote to Cyril to congratulate him as the victor in the controversy, having united the vast majority around his Christology. The Council of Ephesus was certainly a convincing victory for Cyril and his vision of Christology. Although it was not the last word from the early church on this question by some distance, Cyril's work in the furnace of the debate did underpin the significant decisions to be made later at the Council of Chalcedon in 451 and beyond.

As we have begun to see, more than simply tinkering with terminology, Cyril's Christology was about keeping a firm hold on the Scriptural picture not only of Jesus, but of God and the

---

66. For all this, see Hans van Loon, *The Dyophysite Christology of Cyril of Alexandria* (Leiden: Brill, 2009), 531–543.

67. Cyril, Letter 39 in McEnerney, *Letters 1–50*, 147.

salvation He offers in His Son. These are the themes of our next chapters as we look more deeply into Cyril's theology. Like the Apostle Paul centuries before, Cyril saw that when the identity of Jesus Christ is distorted, so is our understanding of God and what it means to know Him – with devastating consequences. 'Another Jesus' goes hand in hand with 'another gospel' (2 Cor. 11:4).

4

GOD: 'GOD CAME DOWN'

A couple of decades before Cyril was born, Athanasius wrote his monumental defence of the gospel against the Arians. The 'Jesus' of the Arians was fundamentally a creature: He was not one being with the Father, nor was He eternal. For Arius and his followers, the self-evident definition of divinity was to be 'ungenerated' or uncaused, and a Son so clearly 'begotten' could never truly qualify as God. He must have come into being later. Athanasius did not only try to correct Arian Christology by showing that the Son was *homoousios* with the Father, but he also dug into the philosophical assumptions behind it. Was beginning with an 'ungenerated' God really a reliable starting point if it forced the exclusion of Jesus the Son? Could a purely philosophical foundation ever accommodate something as category-shattering as the incarnation? So, Athanasius had decided to take on the Arian *doctrine of God*. He wrote that 'it is more pious and more accurate to signify God from the Son and call Him Father, than to name Him from His works only and call Him Unoriginate'. [1] God *is* the creator of all things, and *is* uncreated – of course! – but more basic and important is that God is the *Father* to His Son – and it is in the Son that the

1.   Athanasius, *Against the Arians*, 1.34.

Father has made Himself known. If this is not our starting point in thinking of God, then 'the eternal Son disappears in a puff of philosophy'[2] and with him vanishes any true knowledge of God at all, leaving us with an idol of our own imagination. It is only through the *Son* that we can come to know God as he truly is, not as an abstract Unoriginate being, but as *Father*.

Cyril will have been very familiar with this argument from Athanasius. He knew that the trouble with Arianism was not only a distorted picture of Christ, but a faulty doctrine of God. In the Commentary on John, Cyril seems to echo his predecessor when he writes that 'those who have been called by faith to adoption and eternal life must learn not only that God is one and true but also that he is a Father.'[3] His immersion in the logic of Athanasius' defence against the Arians seemingly served him well as he came to answer the theology of Diodore, Theodore, and Nestorius. Like Athanasius had before him, he could see that the Christology he was taking on had its roots in a doctrine of God that did not begin with the Son, but in philosophical speculation, and therefore bore the rotten fruit of a sub-Christian salvation.

The old 'two schools' theory imagined Theodore and Nestorius coming to their marginal Christology as a result of their distinctive 'Antiochene' biblical exegesis. As we saw in chapter two, though, the reality is that 'theology was the horse and exegesis the cart' for Nestorius and his friends.[4] When Theodore and Nestorius come to explain the reasons for their unique Christology, it is very clear that the 'horse' is a pre-cooked doctrine of God that, like that of the Arians before them, could not properly account for the incarnation – especially the crucifixion.

---

2.   Michael Reeves, *Introducing Major Theologians* (Nottingham: IVP, 2015), 73.

3.   *Jo.* 1:12 in David R. Maxwell, *Commentary on John* (Downers Grove: IVP Academic, 2013), 274.

4.   Donald Fairbairn, 'Patristic Exegesis and Theology: The Cart and the Horse' *Westminster Theological Journal* 69 (2007): 10.

A Horse for Nestorius

The vision of God that Theodore and Nestorius wanted to protect was, in many ways, not controversial or unique. They wanted to preserve the *impassibility* of God (that He is not vulnerable to, or 'moved' by, forces outside Him) and the *immutability* of God (that, in His perfection, He does not change, develop, or 'improve'). These doctrinal commitments were virtually universal in the early church in one form or another, but it seems that, for Theodore and Nestorius, they were given a distinctive shape and content, primarily by the Greek philosopher Aristotle.[5] These convictions – held in this way – meant that, while it is commonly said that Theodore and Nestorius were trying to 'emphasise the full humanity of Christ', their real motivation was to seal off the divine Word from the humanity and the suffering of the man Jesus. The heart of Nestorianism is the 'desire to make clear that the Logos did not suffer or die,' which would, in terms of Aristotelian metaphysics, impinge on His deity.[6]

Brian E. Daley writes that Theodore emphasises 'the *boundaries* between God and creation, between God's sphere of being and activity and that of the concrete, historical world we inhabit.'[7] He quotes Theodore's commentary on the Nicene Creed,

It is well known that the one who is eternal and the one whose existence has a beginning are greatly separated from each other,

5.   For more in immutability and impassibility in the early church, see Thomas G. Weinandy, *Does God Change? The Word's Becoming in the Incarnation* (Still River, MA: St. Bede's, 1985); Weinandy, Does God Suffer? (Notre Dame, IN: University of Notre Dame, 2000); Paul Gavrilyuk, *The Suffering of the Impassable God* (Oxford: OUP, 2004). In broader systematic terms, see Robert Letham, *Systematic Theology* (Wheaton: Crossway, 2019), 165-168.

6.   Fairbairn, *Grace and Christology*, 40. See also, R. P. C. Hanson *The Search for the Christian Doctrine of God* (Edinburgh: T. & T. Clark, 1988) 109-116; and John J. O'Keefe, 'Impassable Suffering? Divine Passion and Fifth Century Christology', *Theological Studies* 58 (1997): 39-60.

7.   Brian E. Daley, *God Visible: Patristic Christology Reconsidered* (Oxford: Oxford University Press, 2018), 178 (emphasis original).

and the gulf found between them is unbridgeable... It is not possible to limit and define the chasm that exists between the one who is from eternity and the one who began to exist at a time when he was not. What possible resemblance and relation can exist between two beings so widely separated from each other?[8]

The concept of a distinction between Creator and creature is, again, nothing new to the early church. But the fixing of an 'unbridgeable' gulf is not a feature of the Nicene theology Theodore attempted to uphold. Athanasius, for example, had emphasised 'the divine Logos's personal, substantial presence *within* the creation as transcendent giver of order and life'.[9] The Son stood where the chasm might have gaped, incarnate, and crucified for sinful creatures. Meanwhile, Theodore was 'mainly concerned to maintain God's *distance*' with the goal of maintaining divine transcendence.[10]

Over and over, Nestorius' writings reveal this agenda, too.[11] His first sermon against *Theotokos* begins with a clear statement of divine providence over (and in contrast to) all the dependent life and circumstances of humanity:

The Creator God, after all, fashioned me in my mother's womb, and he is the first and supreme surety that in those hidden places of the interior I am kept in existence. I am born—and I discover fountains of milk. I begin to experience a need to cut my food in bits, and discover that I am equipped with knives of a sort in my teeth...[12]

Here, God is primarily the Creator, who, of necessity must take care of and rule over creatures, the 'guardian of bodies and

---

8. Daley, *God Visible*, 178.

9. Daley, *God Visible*, 178.

10. Daley, *God Visible*, 178. See also Fairbairn, *Grace and Christology*, 40-42.

11. See O'Keefe, 'Impassable Suffering', 52-54.

12. *Nestorius' First Sermon Against the Theotokos* in Norris, *The Christological Controversy*, 123

souls.'[13] So, Nestorius argues, who could possibly say that *this God* has a human mother? A creature could not produce 'him who is uncreatable', still less could the incarnate God die, but only raise up 'the one in whom he was incarnated', for Christ, as God, is surely 'unaffected by change.'[14] The Creator deity of providence, eternal rule, and no beginning *cannot*, for Nestorius, be identical with the human man who was formed in the womb, endured feet fastened by nails, and was buried in a tomb.[15]

In his reply to Cyril's second letter, in which Cyril speaks of the suffering of the Word, Nestorius wrote:

> to attribute to the Godhead... the properties of the flesh... (and I mean generation, suffering, and death) – then this is either an error of a pagan mentality, brother, or a spirit sick with the madness of Apollinarius or Arius and the other heresies, or something worse.[16]

Later, in the *Book of Heracleides*, he is very concerned about Cyril's use of the communication of idioms, 'making over the things of humanity to the nature and those of the divinity to the nature' (a misunderstanding in any case) and insisting the Word must be 'impassible and immortal and unchangeable'.[17] Nestorius refuses to '*diminish the divinity* by making it passible and mortal.'[18] McGuckin is right that, for Nestorius, 'certain statements were utterly inappropriate for God. God, for example, could not be said to be capable of any passions since he was changeless and self-moving *by definition of being God*.'[19] Similarly, 'to be fully divine means that the Logos can in no sense suffer, be changed,

---

13. Nestorius, 'First Sermon' in Norris, *Controversy*, 123.

14. Nestorius, 'First Sermon' in Norris, *Controversy*, 125–6.

15. Nestorius, 'First Sermon' in Norris, *Controversy*, 129.

16. Nestorius' reply to Cyril's Second Letter, 7 in McGuckin, *The Christological Controversy*, 367.

17. Nestorius, *Herac.* 1.2, 94.

18. Nestorius, *Herac.* 2.1, 185 (emphasis mine).

19. McGuckin, *The Christological Controversy*, 138 (emphasis mine).

limited, or historically relativized in the incarnation.'[20] As Paul B. Clayton puts it, Nestorius sees a 'God who can enter only into prosopic union with us otherwise he would stop being God.'[21]

Cyril believed that Nestorius was allowing human logic to dictate what might be considered fitting and possible for God, without accounting for its fallenness and limitation.[22] Cyril's searching question for this strategy in Theodore and Nestorius is, 'Do you refuse to allow him who is of the holy Virgin his being God and true Son of God the Father? Do you allot suffering to him alone, fending it off from God the Word to avoid God's being declared passible?'[23] 'This', he believes, 'is the point of their pedantic, muddle-headed fictions' and puts them out of step with the 'holy fathers' of Nicaea who believed that Jesus Christ *was* the Word himself.[24]

Robert Jenson writes that Nicene Trinitarianism 'identifies one who underwent gestation, birth, growth, a human career, rejection, torture and execution as "true God"' and that only 'certain Trinitarian affirmations' can allow our theology to hold such apparently counterintuitive thoughts without imposing 'a heavy burden of conceptual dissonance'.[25] Arian Subordinationism, he says, 'relieved the strain by making the one who suffers something less than true God.'[26] But when Nicaea adopted the homoousion and Arianism was ruled out as

20. McGuckin, *The Christological Controversy*, 138.

21. Paul B. Clayton, *The Christology of Theodoret of Cyrus: Antiochene Christology from the Council of Ephesus (431) to the Council of Chalcedon (451)* (Oxford: Oxford University Press, 2007), 288.

22. See McGuckin's excellent introduction to *On the Unity of Christ* (New York: SVS Press, 1995).

23. Cyril, 'On the Creed' in *Cyril of Alexandria: Select Letters*, ed. Lionel Wickham (Oxford: Oxford University Press, 1983), 131.

24. Wickham, *Select Letters*, 131.

25. Robert W. Jenson, *Systematic Theology Volume 1: The Triune God* (Oxford: Oxford University Press, 1997), 125.

26. Jenson, *Systematic Theology*, 125.

an option, 'the dissonance was felt anew.'[27] It was at this point that thinkers like Theodore and Nestorius 'refused to endure the dissonance' and so 'modulated' the identity of Jesus as God the Son, so that when Jesus suffers, God the Son is protected.[28] They were as unwilling as the Arians to have the experience of the incarnate Lord touch His deity. In this way, Jenson says:

> [t]he Antiochene escape is in fact just the Arian escape, moved a notch. The Arians protected God from suffering by distinguishing the suffering Son Jesus from true God. It having now been dogmatically decided that the Son is true God, the Antiochenes protect God by distinguishing the suffering Jesus from the Son. The shielding ontological space between God and the passible Jesus is simply pried open at a different place: at least so far as the divine mark of impassibility is concerned, Jesus must somehow be one thing and God the Son another.[29]

In other words, what has sometimes been called 'Antiochene' theology – Nestorianism – is really modulated Arianism.[30] The concentration on the man Jesus in Nestorius and his friends is not an effort to *honour* the humanity of the Son, but rather, 'motivated by almost frantic passion to protect God from *contamination* by it.'[31]

'Impassible Suffering'

How does Cyril avoid the mistake of Theodore and Nestorius? Is there a way to maintain the doctrines of divine impassibility and immutability and remain thoroughly Nicene? How can the Word be said to suffer?

---

27. Jenson, *Systematic Theology*, 125.

28. Jenson, *Systematic Theology*, 125–126.

29. Jenson, *Systematic Theology*, 126.

30. O'Keefe, too, suggests that the Christological debates of the fifth century were simply an 'unfolding of the implications' of Nicaea ('Impassable Suffering', 57–58).

31. Jenson, *Systematic Theology*, 126, n4 (emphasis mine).

When Cyril speaks about the suffering of Christ, his language is full of subtlety, qualification, and care, because he did believe in impassibility and immutability. Yet he never seeks to distance the eternal Word from humanity, limitations, and suffering in the way that Nestorius did. In his second letter to Nestorius, Cyril wrote:

> So it is we say that he both suffered and rose again; not meaning that the Word of God suffered in his own nature either the scourging or the piercing of the nails, or the other wounds, for the divinity is impassible because it is incorporeal. But in so far as that which had become his own body suffered, then he himself is said to suffer these things for our sake, because the Impassible One was in the suffering body.[32]

While the Word *is* impassible, it was *He* who suffered on the cross: suffering impassibly. This is not sneaky wordplay but, rather, a logical consequence of the hypostatic union and an application of the communication of idioms.[33] For Cyril, the suffering of the Word is always 'in the flesh' (rather than in His divine nature) and it is always 'economic' and undertaken for the sake of our salvation (rather than inflicted incidentally). But the suffering still belongs to the Word. As John McGuckin writes, the flesh 'allowed the Word of God a new condition of expression. In his divine nature he could not possibly suffer, in his human nature he can.'[34] While God cannot suffer in His own nature, the one on the cross *is* none other than 'God-enfleshed-in-history', so God *is* suffering in the flesh that He has made His own. The suffering belongs to the Word made flesh (not God in His nature) and it happens economically, for the sake of salvation – and these two things are 'almost synonymous' in Cyril's mind.[35]

---

32. Cyril, Second Letter to Nestorius, 5 in McGuckin, *The Christological Controversy*, 264.

33. See O'Keefe, 'Impassable Suffering', 57-60.

34. McGuckin, *The Christological Controversy*, 203.

35. See McGuckin, *The Christological Controversy*, 203.

He who endured the noble cross for our sake and tasted of death was no ordinary man conceived of as separate and distinct from the Word of God the Father but it was the Lord of Glory himself who suffered in the flesh, according to the Scriptures (1 Pet. 4.1).[36]

Cyril seems to enjoy and revel in the sense of tension and paradox these statements invite, just as he did *Theotokos*. They were a way to affirm that God had *personally* stepped into the human experience of sin, mortality, and suffering to save us from it. While Nestorius was driven by static philosophical concerns as he defined impassibility, Cyril would not allow those to steamroll over the economy – the reality of what God had *actually done* in Christ. In fact – vitally – the sufferings of Christ do not run *against* the truth about God as something to be explained away or sealed off from Him; instead, for Cyril, the cross *reveals* the glory of God:

The cross is glory. Indeed, at the time of suffering, he patiently and willingly endured many insults that he did not have to suffer. He subjected himself to suffering willingly for us, and undergoing this for the benefit of others is a mark of extreme compassion and the highest glory... The Father is glorified when he shows that he has a Son who is *like he is*... After all, the Father did not give the Son over to death without thinking about it, but *intentionally for the life of the world*.[37]

In Cyril's mind, Jesus Christ shows us who God is precisely *in* the economy of His flesh – and its suffering and death – rather than *despite* it. The self-giving and compassion of the Son on the cross is the 'highest glory' of God, a dazzling showcase of the Father's heart, and the way in which the Father gives life to the

---

36. Cyril, 'Explanation of the Twelve Chapters' 31 in McGuckin, *The Christological Controversy*, 293.

37. Jo. 12:27–28.

world. The sufferings were human and fleshly, but they are a vehicle of divine revelation and divine life.

Nestorius had run from associating the suffering of Christ with God in this way and this indicated that the issue between him and Cyril was not mere Christological terminology. Their dispute was fundamentally a question of whether God is truly present in the world in Christ, or not, and whether God is truly like Jesus, or not. Nestorius could not allow the suffering of the cross to belong to the Son, so had to divert it to another: the assumed man, Jesus. The suffering may have been God's doing in some way, but it was emphatically not the direct experience and action of the Word. Meanwhile, Cyril's conviction was that, however cautious we must be with our language, to remove the suffering of the cross from the Son is lethal to the gospel. If it were not the Son suffering on the cross, then it is not God who came down to save us from our sin and death, but a creature. If it were not the Son suffering on the cross, then the cross has nothing to tell us about God's character. For all the love and compassion we may see there, it was only the death of the assumed man, and there is no insight into what the Son – or His Father – are really like. As it was, Cyril could have sung the old chorus, 'My God is so big, so strong, and so mighty; there's nothing that he cannot do' and he might have added, 'Even suffer in the flesh that is the Word's own!' He did not need Nestorius' glass wall to shield the Word from the suffering of Jesus, because the Word (economically, in His flesh) personally embraced that suffering for us and for our salvation, and so shows us the true love and glory of God.

Cyril Among the Philosophers

Cyril and Nestorius were both committed to the doctrines of impassibility and immutability but seemed to approach them in different ways. For Nestorius and his friends, the terms of engagement seem to have been set by Aristotelian philosophical categories, leading them to conclusions about Jesus that Cyril did not share. Does this mean that Cyril eschewed philosophy altogether? What really distinguished Cyril's approach from that of Nestorius? It will help us to understand the delicate relationship early Christian writers had with Greek philosophy.

In the nineteenth century, F. C. Baur proposed that the purity of early Christianity had been compromised by the incoming of Greek metaphysics. He believed this pollution began in the New Testament writings as the apostles Paul and Luke 'Hellenized' the Hebraic traditions of Peter and James.[38] For Baur, the result of this syncretism was 'Catholicism': a kind of necessary evil if the new religion were to work in any Gentile setting. When Harnack later took up Baur's theory (and coined the term 'Hellenization'),[39] he viewed the marriage as even more sinister, creating alien 'dogma': 'a work of the Greek spirit on the soil of the Gospel.'[40] Downstream from Baur and Harnack, modern theologians occasionally fall into telling a rather simplistic story in which the original Hebrew essence of the faith was quickly diluted by Greek metaphysics, resulting in extra-Scriptural systems of doctrine, inventions in language (like 'hypostasis' or 'Trinity'), and that only a recovery of a pristine, non-philosophical golden age could rescue 'true Christianity'.

---

38. See Ferdinand Christian Baur, *History of Christian Dogma* [ed. Peter C. Hodgson, trans. Peter C. Hodgson and Robert F. Brown] (Oxford: Oxford University Press, 2014).

39. Daniel Geese, 'The Similarity of the Two Masters' in *Ferdinand Christian Baur and the History of Early Christianity* [eds. Martin Bauspiess, Christof Landmesser, and David Lincicum; trans. Robert F. Brown and Peter. C. Hodgson] (Oxford: Oxford University Press, 2017), 361.

40. Harnack, *History of Dogma* vol. I, 17. For an astute assessment of Harnack's take on the Hellenization theory, see Christoph Markschies, 'Does It Make Sense to Speak about a "Hellenization of Christianity" in Antiquity?', Church History and Religious Culture 92, 1 (2012): 5–34 and *Hellenisierung des Christentums: Sinn und Unsinn einer Historischen Deutungskategorie* (Leipzig: Evangelische Verlagsanstalt, 2012), as well as the earlier *The 'Hellenization' of Judea in the First Century After Christ* (SCM Press, 1989) by Martin Hengel in collaboration with Markschies.

Yet the reality of the relationship between early Christianity and philosophy was, as Lewis Ayers puts it, 'a complex and piecemeal affair between Christian, Jewish, and Greek and Roman philosophical traditions.'[41] In fact, R. L. Wilken argues that, as Christianity came to inhabit Greco-Roman thought and culture, *it* transformed *them* into something new altogether.[42] It is possible that Wilken slightly over-eggs the cake, not emphasising enough the ways in which the early church *did*, at times, see that Greek metaphysics could dangerously threaten the gospel.[43] Clearly, though, it is too ham-fisted to look at early church writers and ask whether they were 'infected' by philosophy or had remained untainted. No theological thinker is ever totally independent of those who have gone before them, shaping concepts, language, and arguments – whether Christian or pagan. It is not always straightforward to pick apart how any thinker is shaped by their various influences. Early Christians believed that the ancient philosophers were 'squinting at the truth', as E. P. Meijering says, which makes it possible to start a discussion with them in which they may be praised or attacked, depending on their proximity to Christian beliefs.[44] Cyril, like many of the early church writers, believed, for example, that Plato's best ideas were actually borrowed from the Hebrew Scriptures.[45] By engaging Greek philosophy in this way, the early

---

41. Lewis Ayers, *Nicaea and its Legacy* (Oxford: Oxford University Press, 2004), 391. Mark Edwards refers to 'the uneasy, though unavoidable, integration of theology with philosophy in early Christian literature.' Mark Edwards, *Aristotle and Early Christian Thought* (London: Routledge, 2019), x.

42. Robert Louis Wilken, *The Spirit of Early Christian Thought* (New Haven: Yale University Press, 2003), xv–xvii.

43. This was the concern of Paul in 1 Cor 1:20–25 where the Greeks' concern for philosophical wisdom risked obscuring the power of God in the cross of Christ. It was the concern of Irenaeus as he countered Valentinian Gnosticism. It was the concern of Athanasius as he sought to displace Arius' God Unoriginate with the Father of Jesus Christ.

44. Meijering, 'Platontists and the Trinity', 17.

45. See E. P. Meijering, 'Cyril of Alexandria on the Platontists and the Trinity' in *Nederlands Theologisch Tijdschrift* 28 (1974): 16–29. A classic early example is Justin

church 'baptised' its metaphysics, pressing it into the service of the gospel. The question seems to be: how well did the early theologians manage their relationship with the philosophical thought of their day? Who could adopt (and, where necessary, challenge) the likes of Plato, Aristotle, and others so that their thought *served* the gospel of Christ? And who, on the other hand, allowed pagan thought into the driving seat, undermining a truly *Christian* theology?

Cyril is a fascinating case study in all this. He has not generally been regarded as a master of the philosophical language and concepts of his day.[46] Lionel Wickham wrote that Cyril was little more than a 'careful amateur' when it came to philosophy, being unable to boast a deep engagement with Aristotle.[47] At times, Cyril's use of Christological language is not as consistent as a keen philosopher might hope (Wickham actually says he made 'a pig's breakfast' of it!).[48] On the other hand, Ruth Siddals and Hans

---

Martyr, who wrote, 'Plato likewise borrowed from Moses when, while inquiring into the nature of the Son of God in the *Timaeus*, he states "He places him in the universe in the manner of the letter X." For, in the writings of Moses it is stated that, at the time when the Israelites left Egypt and were living in the desert, they encountered poisonous beasts, vipers, asps, and every sort of serpent which brought death to the people, and that Moses, through the inspiration and impulse of God, took some brass, shaped it into the figure of a cross, placed it over the holy tabernacle, and announced to the people, "If you gaze upon this figure and believe, you shall be saved thereby." (...) When Plato read this, he did not clearly understand it, for, not perceiving that the figure of the cross was spoken of, he took it for the form of the letter X, and said that the power next to the first God was placed into the universe in the form of the letter X.' Justin Martyr, *Writings of Saint Justin Martyr*, trans. Thomas B. Falls, FaCh vol. 6 (New York: Christian Heritage, 1948), 97–98 (*First Apology* 60).

46. Hans van Loon, *The Dyophysite Theology of Cyril of Alexandria* (Leiden: Brill, 2009), 62–65. Ironically, Harnack believed that Alexandrian theologians like Cyril were the most philosophically-driven of the early church writers, concerned with their systems of soteriology, especially influenced by Platonism. (Harnack, *History of Dogma* vol. IV, 139, fn 1.)

47. Lionel Wickham, 'La paradoxe trinitaire chez Cyrille Herméneutique, analyses philosophiques théologique. By Marie-Odile Boulnois', *Journal of Theological Studies*, 48, no. 1 (1997): 289.

48. Wickham, 'La paradoxe trinitaire', 289.

van Loon have argued that Cyril quite capably deploys the tools of Aristotelian logic, distinctions, and definitions to good effect in his arguments in the *Thesaurus* and *Dialogues on the Trinity*.[49] He claims Aristotle as an inspiration in precision and accuracy with terminology, and even accuses one opponent of incompetence in 'the Aristotelian art'.[50] He clearly does not eschew Aristotle, but neither is he a blind devotee. He criticises opponents for attacking him 'on the basis of Aristotle's teachings', making 'full use of the cleverness of worldly wisdom', and so, counting as nothing their propensity to stray from orthodox doctrine.[51] His posture towards Greek philosophy, Wickham says, was akin to 'brief pillaging expeditions, as it were, into enemy country, after which he is content to retreat' to biblical exegesis and trinitarian theology where he is really most at home.[52] Cyril might not have welcomed this allusion, but there is booty to be plundered from the Egyptians as the people of God make their way to the Promised Land and, so long as it does not become a golden calf, it can be valuable to us.

For Cyril, it is the Scriptural doctrine of the triune God which ought to be the church's theological starting point, as the Son of God unveils the Father. Philosophical thought may be an aid in structuring and communicating all this, but Scripture – recording the actual facts of God's presence with, and revelation to, humanity – cannot be supplanted or undermined by prefabricated ideas. This was where Cyril and Nestorius really differed. Their conflict emerges, says O'Keefe,

---

49.   Ruth Siddals, "Logic and Christology in Cyril of Alexandria', *Journal of Theological Studies* 38 no. 2 (1987): 341-367 and Hans van Loon, *The Dyophysite Theology of Cyril of Alexandria* (Leiden: Brill, 2009), 62-122.

50.   Mark Edwards, *Aristotle and Early Christian Thought* (London: Routledge, 2019), 89-92.

51.   Hans van Loon, *The Dyophysite Theology of Cyril of Alexandria* (Leiden: Brill, 2009), 94. Loon is quoting from *Thesaurus* 145B and Dial. Trin. II, 418C.

52.   Wickham, 'La paradoxe trinitaire', 289.

when the scriptural narrative collides with certain philosophical pre-suppositions about what God can and cannot be like. In my view, Cyril wanted to say that when philosophy and the biblical narrative conflict, preference ought to be given to the biblical narrative. The Antiochenes tended to do the reverse.[53]

Cyril on the Trinity

Cyril felt that, although Nestorius *claimed* adherence to the Nicene Creed, his theological and philosophical foundations meant that confession was hollow. Cyril wanted to protect both the letter and the *spirit* of the Creed against Nestorianism.[54] He believed that his letters to Nestorius were the 'necessary interpretive key for unlocking the true teaching of the Creed' and rightly understanding its portrait of Christ, the salvation He offered, and the Father who sent Him.[55] The church was still seeking clarity on all this, and Cyril's interventions played a significant part in settling the picture.[56] Cyril's theological baseline, which he believed he inherited from Nicaea and Athanasius, was that God is fundamentally a Father giving life to the Son in the Holy Spirit.[57]

This truth is not simply understood by the human inquirer: 'I assume that every mind on earth is totally inadequate for an accurate exposition of these matters.'[58] But it is 'heavenly

---

53. John O'Keefe, 'Impassable Suffering', 41.

54. 'And in no manner do we permit the defined faith to be shaken by anyone, or the creed of the faith, defined by our holy Fathers who assembled at Nicaea in critical times. Nor, indeed, do we allow, either by us or by others, either a word to be changed in it or a single syllable to be omitted...' Cyril, *Ep.* 39.7.

55. Mark S. Smith, *The Idea of Nicaea in the Early Church Councils*, AD 431–451 (Oxford: Oxford University Press, 2018), 210.

56. Smith, *The Idea of Nicaea*, 209–214.

57. At the end of Ep. 39, he defends Athanasius against an alleged forgery of a letter of his by Nestorius, which had rendered it unorthodox. See McEnerney, *Letters* 1–50, 152.

58. *Jo.* 14:20.

treasure' for those who will dig into Scripture.[59] Cyril is wary of any impertinent delving into the workings of the Trinity, going beyond what is written, and is driven less by the desire to pin down the 'what' and 'how' so much as the desire to worship God in truth.[60] This means that he has a constant focus on the revelation of the Father through the Son in the Spirit. In his commentary on Luke 10:22, he says:

> Only the Holy and consubstantial Trinity knows itself, only the Trinity, which is beyond all human words and understanding. But the Son through the Holy Spirit unveils the Trinity.[61]

This direct revelation by the Son is possible because the Son is eternally of the being of the Father, and the Father does all that he does *through* the Son, *in* the Spirit.[62] In fragmentary comments on Luke's Gospel, Cyril writes:

> [the Son] has been called the hand and arm of God the Father, since he [i.e., the Father] does all things through him [i.e., the Son], and the Son similarly works by the Spirit. Therefore, just as the finger is dependent on the hand, as something that is not foreign to it, but in it by nature, so also the Holy Spirit is joined into unity with the Son by reason of his consubstantiality, even though he proceeds from God the Father. For, as I said, the Son does everything through the consubstantial Spirit.[63]

The Father, Son, and Holy Spirit dwell within one another and do not merely 'co-operate' as three individual gods could. Instead, they do all that they do inseparably, for 'all things are

---

59. From the preface to the Thesaurus, quoted by Marie-Odile Boulnois in *The Theology of St. Cyril of Alexandria: A Critical Appreciation*, edited by Thomas Weinandy, and Daniel Keating (London: Bloomsbury, 2003), 79.

60. Weinandy and Keating, *Theology of St. Cyril*, 80.

61. *Luc.* 10:22 (PG 72, 673a), quoted in Weinandy and Keating, *Theology of St. Cyril*, 82.

62. See Matthew R. Crawford, *Cyril of Alexandria's Trinitarian Theology of Scripture* (Oxford: Oxford University Press, 2014).

63. *Fragments* on Luke 141, quoted in Matthew R. Crawford, *Cyril of Alexandria's Trinitarian Theology of Scripture*, 51.

from the Father, through the Son, in the Spirit and the holy and consubstantial Trinity is glorified in all things that are accomplished'.[64] As well as guarding against tritheism, Cyril's commentary on John argues against the idea that the Son has only a 'relational union' with the Father, where 'the Son is loved by the Father and he loves the Father in return'. This language could easily accommodate Arianism, in which the Son may be very much loved, yet is 'not at all in the essence of God the Father but is completely distinct from him'. Were this the case, the Son would not be a true son, and the Father not a true father, and these names and their relationship would only exist 'by the law of love'.

To Cyril, this would seem a dangerously surface-level kind of oneness. He argues that, yes, the Father and Son share in perfect loving relationship, but the Son is in the Father *by nature*, not only through some shared affection.[65] The Son is not a separate being who can either attract or forfeit the love of the Father; he is first of all the *Father's eternally begotten Son* and, for that reason, mutual love is the beautiful characteristic of their life together. The salvation of humanity relies upon this. If the Son is not from the being of the Father, 'the famous wonder of the Father's love will finally come to nothing because he exchanged a creature for creatures and not truly his Son.'[66] The Son must not only be in a loving relationship *with* God, but truly *be* Himself 'God from God' who is 'naturally joined to God the Father' and 'from the substance of God the Father'. This way, even as He is joined to humanity in the incarnation, He has the Father in Himself, and is, in turn, in the Father. Only in this way can He bring His own eternal life and His own loving Father to us who believe.[67]

---

64. Cyril, *Commentary on 1 Corinthians* 12:7ff in P. E. Pusey (ed.), *Sancti patris nostri Cyrilli archiepiscopi Alexandrini in D. Joannis evangelium*, vol. 3 (Oxford: Clarendon Press, 1872), 287–288.

65. *Jo.* 14:20.

66. *Jo.* 3:16.

67. *Jo.* 14:20.

The Son, Cyril says, 'shines forth from the Father's essence' and shares His attributes, showing the Father in the way the sun's rays are really *from* and *part of* the sun, though distinct from it; or the way a sweet aroma comes from fragrant herbs.[68] Knowing the Son in this way, we are able to see and know the Father as the begetter of the Son. 'The Father and the Son are together since he is and is understood to be Father because he is known to have begotten [the Son].'[69] The Son is the route to the truest and deepest knowledge of God because the Son is essential to the Father. In fact, he writes, 'Father' is a better way to speak of God than simply calling Him 'God':

> God (...) is not a Father in name only, but he has his own offspring in himself and from himself, concurrent with and coeternal with his own nature. (...) And God's name *Father* is more proper than the name *God*. The one signifies honor, but the other signifies his essential attribute. When someone uses the word *God*, they are referring to the Lord of all. But when someone uses the word *Father*, they are touching on the definition of what belongs to his person, since they have made it known that he has begotten.[70]

Like Athanasius, Cyril saw that our ability to pray 'Our Father' rests on the nature of the Father-Son relationship. This privilege rests on the fact that God truly and eternally *is* Father by nature and is shared with us by His own Son who is His image and radiance (Heb 1:3). We will return to this in the next chapter.

The Eternal Son

Cyril's focus on the Trinity is evident in his reading of the Old Testament as much as the New. He considered the Hebrew Scriptures to be as clear a guide to the triunity of God as the Gospels since God has always been the Father of the Son,

68. *Jo.* 14:20.

69. *Jo.* 17:3.

70. *Jo.* 17:6–8.

and the Son has always made Him known – whether after the incarnation or before it. He therefore stands in a long tradition of patristic writers who identify the Son as active in the Old Testament in theophanies, so that all of Scripture centres on Him. McGuckin writes,

> The patristic writers... regard the text as a continuous narrative of the Logos himself. It was the Word who spoke through all the prophets, the Word who inspired the psalms, the Word who appeared to Abraham, Moses, and Jacob, and so on. In every instance the text (be it Old or New Testament) relates to the Logos' revelation of God, whether in the life of the Trinity or the earthly economy of salvation... This thoroughgoing christocentricity, and the different understanding of historical reality, marks off their exegesis from contemporary interpreters (...)[71]

When Cyril comments on the Old Testament narrative, he sees it as being straightforwardly *about* Christ. His commentary on Isaiah 7 argues that the prophet was not speaking about the birth of Hezekiah (something which, later, could retrospectively be applied to Christ by the New Testament writers). Instead, Isaiah directly foresaw the birth of Christ from a virgin: 'you will call his name Emmanuel, that is, you will acknowledge that God has appeared in human form.'[72] His writing is deeply typological or 'spiritual', often seeing the text's foreshadowing of the incarnation and the passion of Christ, even outside of the direct prophecies. When he mentions the dimensions of Noah's ark in length, width, and height, he says that its construction 'signified the mystery of Christ'. This ought to be 'completely and utterly obvious', he says, to anyone who has read Paul's prayer that believers might know 'the breadth, and the height,

---

71. McGuckin, *The Christological Controversy*, 190.

72. *Commentary on Isaiah.* 7:14-16 in Russell, *Cyril of Alexandria*, 79.

and the length and the depth, and to know the love of Christ which surpasses knowledge' (Eph 3:18-19).[73]

Beyond this, like many of his forebears, he also identifies the Word as the one who wrestled with Jacob (a 'man' who is 'the face of God' and 'true God').[74] Daniel's vision of the Son of Man (Dan 7) is a vision of 'Emmanuel' in which the Word appears '*like* a Son of Man', distinguished from humanity in His divine nature, and yet, since He is the only begotten Word of God, He receives the honour and service of the whole creation *while in His manhood*.[75] It was the Word who delivered the Israelites with Moses (the 'strong hand and outstretched arm' of Ps 136:12) and the Word who promised to be with Joshua as He was with Moses (Josh 3:7).[76] His Hebrews commentary identifies 'the Son Himself' as the Spiritual Rock of Israel, the Lord who appeared to Amos standing on a wall, and the Lord of Hosts enthroned in Isaiah.[77] Cyril believes it was Christ who descended on Mount Sinai in the form of fire in Exodus 19.[78] When Jesus tells the Jewish leaders that Abraham had rejoiced to see His day (John 8:58), it was in part because Abraham had foreseen the death of Christ in his own offering of Isaac (Gen. 22), but also because Christ 'was known even to their most ancient fathers, since he is eternal'.[79] Cyril, therefore, considers the Son to be the object of saving faith for the patriarchs as much as for New Testament believers. Abraham, he writes, was made righteous 'through

---

73. *Glaphyra on the Pentateuch volume 1,* Fathers of the Church 137, Nicholas P. Lunn and Gregory K. Hillis eds. (Washington DC: Catholic University of America Press, 2018), 93.

74. *Scholia on the Incarnation* 31, in John McGuckin, *The Christological Controversy of Alexandria,* 326.

75. *Scholia on the Incarnation* 32 (emphasis mine). Daniel thus sees ahead to the incarnation.

76. *On the Unity of Christ,* trans. John A. McGuckin (New York: SVS Press, 1995), 52–53.

77. *Commentary on Hebrews,* trans. Khach'ik Grigoryan (Yerevan: Ankyunacar Publishing, 2021) 33–35.

78. *Jo.* 14:9.

79. *Jo.* 8:58.

faith alone in Christ' set free from sin by 'Christ himself, who justifies.'[80] Rather than believing in 'God' in some general sense, the faithful saints of the Hebrew Scriptures specifically trusted in Christ, and so knew God and received eternal life. Cyril writes:

> It was likely that some who engaged in Jewish rather than evangelical learning thought that the confession and knowledge of the one God of all was sufficient for right faith, and they were not interested in learning the doctrine about the holy and consubstantial Trinity. Consequently, Christ excludes those who think this way from the knowledge of God unless they should be willing to accept him. Access to God the Father comes through the Son.[81]

In all this, Cyril is careful to draw a distinction between the Son's many visits to the prophets and saints in the Hebrew Scriptures and the entirely unique incarnation of the Word in the New Testament.[82] The incarnation gives believers 'a better way than that given to the ancients' that goes beyond manifestations of God to Him being our *possession* in Christ.[83] Identifying various appearances of the Son does not undermine or relativise the importance of His coming in the flesh, though. In fact, these appearances cause the incarnation to ring true for those who read the Scriptures rightly. The various titles applied to the Son during His ministry in the Old Testament can rightly be attributed to the man Jesus Christ because He is the exact same person.

> (...) he became man like us, even though the same one who economically came to assume flesh and blood, also remained unalterably and unchangeably in his own proper nature. It is one person that the god-inspired scripture (both before and

---

80. Jo. 8:34.
81. Jo. 14:7.
82. Jo. 1:14.
83. Jo. 14:9.

after the incarnation) designates as, Only Begotten, Word, God, Image, Radiance, and Impress of the Father's Very Being, Life, Glory, Light, Wisdom, Power, Strong Right Hand, Most High, Magnificence, Lord of Hosts, and other such names which are truly fitting for the deity. And similarly one person (after the incarnation) that it calls, Man, Jesus Christ, Atonement, Mediator, First Fruits of the Dead, First Born From the Dead, Second Adam, and Head of the Body that is the Church. Both sets of titles apply to him. All are his, the first series as well as those which apply in these last times of this age.

He is one therefore, who was true God before the incarnation, and even in the manhood remained what He was, and is, and shall be (...) we say that Jesus Christ is one and the same, even though we recognise the difference of the natures and keep them unconfused with each other.[84]

This sort of Old Testament exegesis is not to be found in Diodore, Theodore, and Nestorius. This is notable because it is not an 'Alexandrian' option as opposed to their 'Antiochene' option, but almost universal in the early church. Unlike the majority of the early church theologians, these three did not treat the Old Testament as Christian literature. Behr says that, for Diodore and Theodore, for example, the Psalms 'do not speak of Christ, for David belongs to the narrative stream of "the old age" rather than "the new age" of Christ, which has its own narrative.'[85] At the Second Council of Constantinople in 553, Theodore was accused of expunging Christ from the Old Testament Scriptures, and instead attributing the Psalms 'in Jewish fashion' to 'the circles around Zerubbabel and Hezekiah' and denied that all but three of the Psalms were messianic or Christocentric.[86] He interpreted them in a way more consistent with rabbinic monotheism ('in Jewish fashion') than with

---

84. *Scholia on the Incarnation*, 13.

85. Behr, *Diodore and Theodore*, 41.

86. Behr, *Diodore and Theodore*, 35.

Trinitarian Christianity. For Diodore and Theodore, 'the Old Testament Scriptures, with scant exception, did not speak of Christ.'[87]

Nestorius wrote that God could not have appeared in the Old Testament. The theophany of the burning bush was, he says, an angel appearing 'as' God and speaking on His behalf. He reasons that this isn't a lie or a contradiction because, while the angel is not technically God, God is said to be there 'by means of' the angel. It is a kind of mediated presence of God in a creature.[88] It is hard not to see here an analogy of his Christology. In the incarnation, too, God was not present in the world *directly* as the Word in flesh, but 'by means of' His arrangement with the assumed man, Jesus, a creature. Perhaps, had Nestorius seen God the Son in the Hebrew Scriptures, he would have been prepared to identify God the Son directly in the incarnation.

Nearly two hundred years before, Tertullian had written that Christ's appearances on the Old Testament were the Son 'learning' and 'rehearsing' for the incarnation – both for His own preparation, and to

> level for us the way of faith, that we might the more readily believe that the Son of God had come down into the world, if we knew that in times past also something similar had been done.[89]

This was the common understanding of many of the fathers. For here, in the Old Testament, was the Son *before His incarnation* content to be laughed at by Sarah (Gen 18:15), physically overpowered by Jacob (Gen 32:26), and held in ignorant suspicion by Moses (Exod 3:13) – just as later, in His flesh, He

---

87. Behr, *Diodore and Theodore*, 37.

88. *Book of Heracleides*, 1.1.56, 53.

89. Tertullian, *Against Praxeas*, 16, in *Latin Christianity: Its Founder, Tertullian*, ed. Alexander Roberts, James Donaldson, and A. Cleveland Coxe, trans. Peter Holmes, vol. 3, The Ante-Nicene Fathers (Buffalo, NY: Christian Literature Company, 1885).

would be mocked by the impenitent thief (Luke 23:39), beaten by soldiers (Mark 15:15), and rejected by Israel (John 5:40). Here was Jesus Christ *before His incarnation* enthroned on the Mercy Seat (Ps 99:1) and ascended to heaven in flame from the altar of sacrifice (Judg 13:20) – just as later, in His flesh, He would be glorified on the cross (John 12:32) and offer Himself as a sacrifice for the sin of the world (Heb 1:3).

When Irenaeus had written against the Gnostics, centuries before, he was at pains to show that the gospel was lost if there was not *one* God, with *one* plan of salvation, revealed in *one* unified Scriptural message, in both Old and New Testament. Diodore, Theodore, and Nestorius undoubtedly fell into the same trap as the Gnostics. Their division of *Scripture* was as radical as the division they saw in *Christ*. The main reason for it is that they did not straightforwardly identify the man Jesus Christ as identical with the eternal Word. They did not see the incarnate Lord *precisely* as the one who had previously dwelt with the Father, appeared to Abraham, and now enfleshed. 'Christ', for them, is simply not a reality in the Old Testament texts; He had not been born yet. If the Father's Word – His revelation of Himself – is not the same through all history, then there can be no real unity to Scripture. The link between the exegesis and the Christology is virtually inseparable, and the Church condemned Nestorianism for both things together.[90]

Nestorius's deepest problem was that he had his definition of God prepared long before he came to look at the Son, whether in the Old Testament or New.[91] The carpenter from Nazareth, in the manger and on the cross, was never going to fit with his understanding of God.[92] It meant that the unified witness of

---

90. See Behr, *Diodore and Theodore*, 35.

91. See Paul B. Clayton, *The Christology of Theodoret of Cyrus: Antiochene Christology from the Council of Ephesus (431) to the Council of Chalcedon (451)* (Oxford: Oxford University Press, 2007), 286–288; McGuckin, *The Christological Controversy*, 138.

92. So, John O'Keefe: 'Christian theology, in particular Christology, should pay attention to the particular words that narrate to us the story of salvation. Cyril

Scripture to God's triunity were missing in his theology, and could not shape his gospel, as we will see in the next chapter. Cyril, on the other hand, saw the knowledge of God going out in the same way at all points throughout redemptive history: the Father revealing Himself in the Son and through the Holy Spirit. The Son is *the way* the Father has given to know Him to all believers through all time, and so is the unavoidable centre of all Scripture and the unchanging object of saving faith.[93] The revelation of the Father in the Son in the Spirit-inspired Scriptures is the beating heart of salvation, from the fall to the last day.

Getting God and Humanity in the Same Room

At the heart of this chapter has been the doctrine of God and the way which we are to begin our thinking about speaking about Him. Nestorius and his friends could not speak rightly about the incarnation because of their starting point in an abstractly philosophical doctrine of God. In the next chapter, we will see that they struggled to paint a picture of God and humanity in any close relationship at all. On the other hand, Cyril began with the eternal Son who makes the Father known. He could therefore speak of Christ as *God Himself* touching our world and our very humanity. Hard as it is to comprehend, the impassible, immutable, and eternal God has truly come to be with us in Christ and makes real relationship possible.

> *The Word who is God came down out of heaven* and entered our likeness, that is to say submitted to birth from a woman

recognized in those narratives shocking claims about the fullness of God's participation with us in the concrete person of Jesus. He understood that those narratives provide the grammar of Christian discourse, and that to those narratives other convictions, for example the impassibility of God, should be subordinate. Nestorius and Theodoret backed away from the implications of the Incarnation. Cyril did not.' (O'Keefe, 'Impassible Suffering', 58.)

93. See Matthew R. Crawford, *Cyril of Alexandria's Trinitarian Theology of Scripture* (Oxford: Oxford University Press), 2014, for a good study on the Son's place in Scripture.

according to the flesh, while ever remaining what he was, that is one from on high... Indeed the mystery of Christ runs the risk of being disbelieved *precisely because it is so incredibly wonderful.* For God was in humanity. He who was above all creation was in our human condition; the invisible one was made visible in the flesh; he who is from the heavens and from on high was in the likeness of earthly things; the immaterial one could be touched; he who is free in his own nature came in the form of a slave; he who blesses all creation became accursed; he who is all righteousness was numbered among transgressors; life itself came in the appearance of death. All this followed because the body which tasted death belonged to no other but to him who is the Son by nature.[94]

Brian Daley says that Cyril's writings resist 'any theological position that would weaken the identification of Jesus or the Spirit with the transcendent God' and so emphasise 'the saving, life-giving, immediate presence of that God, through Jesus and the Spirit, within history and at the heart of the Church's daily life'.[95] It is this question of the 'immediate presence of God' that kept Nestorius and Cyril at such a distance from one another, as it played out in Christology.

Unlike Nestorius, Cyril was able to get God and humanity together in the same room – because of the incarnation. The Nestorian doctrine of God did not allow humanity and divinity truly to meet, either in the person of Christ or, thereby, in the salvation of Christians. God could not truly have humanity, and neither could humanity truly have God. For Cyril, though, fellowship between divine and human *is* possible for us now because the two have already been perfectly joined in one person: Jesus Christ. He writes that Christ is the mediator between God and man, joining humanity to God 'through himself and in himself'. This He can do because He first 'sprang from the substance of God the Father... being completely in the Father

---

94. Cyril, *On the Unity of Christ*, 61 (emphasis mine).

95. Weinandy and Keating, *Theology of Cyril*, 129.

and having the Father in him' *and also*, because 'he became human like us, he joins himself with those on earth (but not with our sin) and has become a kind of borderland, containing in himself the elements that concur in unity and friendship.'[96]

As John O'Keefe puts it, Nestorius' Christology means that 'the divine rests safely isolated from the human, tucked up in heaven and transcendent.' So, 'one wonders now as Cyril wondered then, are we saved? ... Has God touched the world at all?' While Cyril, 'albeit with plenty of qualification, announced that God's presence in Christ was unmediated and direct: Jesus is the "one incarnate nature of the Word." Jesus is the second person of the Trinity.'[97]

In Cyril's theology, since one of the Trinity has come to share in the life of the world in the incarnation, the world is able to share in the life of the Trinity. Since God has made Himself present to us in Jesus, we are able to be present in the eternal love and fellowship of Father, Son, and Spirit. The incarnation of the Son is not incidental with God, but the very means by which He gives *Himself to us* and draws *us to Himself*. The person and work of Christ on earth are not a passing phase or a brief chapter in the Son's existence, after which He returned to being aloof and transcendently other. Jesus' incarnate and very human experiences of pain, suffering, and death, borne on our behalf, cannot be ejected from God's life because, in the economy of His flesh, they are really His. They cannot be separated from Him, and we cannot imagine Him without them. There is no other 'son' or 'god' in heaven except this one who has come to us in such astonishing kindness and goodness. We can perhaps agree with Paul B. Clayton who comments that the

> biblical God who cares, who enters into human pain and suffering[...] The God who can remain who he is, who can remain God, whose eternalness and being are not threatened

---

96. *Jo.* 14:6.
97. O'Keefe, 'Impassable Suffering', 58.

by anything seen or unseen, but who can take into his own life all that is truly human, enter himself into our history—Cyril's Word—is to me infinitely more appealing than the God who can enter only into prosopic union with us otherwise he would stop being God.[98]

In all His humanity the man Jesus – God the Son – perfectly expresses and embodies the being and life of the Father to us and for us. He is fully and faithfully Himself, and turned unswervingly towards us in love.

---

98.   Paul B. Clayton, *Theodoret*, 288.

5

SALVATION: 'LOVED AS SONS'

Cyril's insistence on a unitive Christology – a specific understanding of the identity of Jesus Christ – was not driven by the desire to fight with Nestorius and his colleagues. Cyril was not simply trying to defend 'orthodox theology' in some abstract sense. Neither was he interested in pushing a certain method of biblical interpretation. What drove Cyril's Christology and his reading of Scripture was an understanding of how God graciously relates to humanity: it was a particular view of salvation.

Partakers of the Divine Nature

Like many of the theologians of his day, Cyril stood self-consciously in a long stream of thought that saw salvation as the believer's union with God. Rather than God simply doing something *to* or *for* a believer from a distance (such as forgiving their sin or granting them entrance to heaven), the early church thought of salvation as God drawing us into his own life to enjoy intimate fellowship with him.[1] Believers in Jesus are united to

---

1. See Daniel A. Keating, *The Appropriation of Divine Life in Cyril of Alexandria* (Oxford University Press, 2000) and *Deification and Grace* (Catholic University of American Press, 2007); Norman Russell, *The Doctrine of Deification in the Greek Patristic Tradition* (Oxford University Press, 2004); Ben C. Blackwell, *Christosis: Pauline Soteriology in the Light of Deification in Irenaeus and Cyril of Alexandria* (Tübingen: Mohr Siebeck, 2011);Vladimir Kharlamov, 'Theosis in Patristic Thought', *Theology*

him in *his* life, now filled with *his* Holy Spirit and able to call *his* Father '*our* Father'. In baptism, the believer has died and been raised with Christ to live a new kind of life by faith in him (Gal 2:20). They are no longer defined by the old life of sin and death in Adam but come to know true life by God's grace (Rom 6:1-11). And this life is not something new God invents for the purpose of salvation: it is specifically *Jesus Christ's* life, opened to Christians. The reason the eternal Son of God took our human nature was to give us a share in his *own* eternal life (John 17:3).

Irenaeus of Lyons, writing against the Gnostics in the second century put it this way:

> the Word of God, our Lord Jesus Christ... did, through His transcendent love, become what we are, that He might bring us to be even what He is Himself.[2]

After him, Athanasius, writing against the Arians, famously explained, 'He, indeed, assumed humanity that we might become God.'[3] Athanasius' statement seems, on the face of it, to go further than Irenaeus' does – perhaps further than we might feel comfortable with. Can it be right to say that we 'become God'? This understanding of salvation has been called *theosis* or 'deification' and has raised serious questions for theologians over the centuries. Is it biblical and accurate to speak of salvation

Today Volume 65 (2008): 158-168; Jared Ortiz (ed.) *Deification in the Latin Patristic Tradition* (Catholic University of America Press, 2019); David Meconi, *The One Christ: St Augustine's Theology of Deification* (Catholic University of America Press, 2013); Paul M. Collins, *Partaking in the Divine Nature: Deification and Communion* (T&T Clark, 2010).

2. Irenaeus of Lyons, *Against Heresies*, Preface to Book V, in *The Apostolic Fathers with Justin Martyr and Irenaeus*, ed. Alexander Roberts, James Donaldson, and A. Cleveland Coxe, vol. 1, The Ante-Nicene Fathers (Buffalo, NY: Christian Literature Company, 1885).

3. Athanasius of Alexandria, *On the Incarnation*, trans. a religious of C.S.M.V. (New York: SVS Press, 1996), 93.

in these terms?[4] We should note that Irenaeus, Athanasius, and others had in mind several Scriptural texts which speak quite boldly about the reality of the life of the believer:

> He has granted to us his precious and very great promises, so that through them *you may become partakers of the divine nature*, having escaped from the corruption that is in the world. (2 Peter 1:4)

> I said, "You are gods,
>   sons of the Most High, all of you. (Psalm 86:2)

Just as God the Son came to share in *our* nature, we are brought to be 'partakers of the *divine* nature', as 'sons of the Most High', in union with him. The point here is not that believers cease to be creatures and are somehow absorbed into the eternal being of God, nor that God is somehow expanded beyond the persons of the Trinity to include multitudes more in a kind of pagan pantheon. This is never what the early church theologians meant to imply. Deification is a transformation of the *manner* or *mode* of our existence, not its substance, because we remain what we are, and God remains what He is. Nevertheless, we *do* come to participate in God and His life: and we do so *as creatures* and *in a creaturely way,* by his grace.[5] Salvation is not something we receive at a distance from God, served up with a long-handled spoon; neither is it a blurring of our humanity into a kind of divinity –

---

4.   Ben C. Blackwell, *Christosis: Pauline Soteriology in the Light of Deification in Irenaeus and Cyril of Alexandria* (Tübingen: Mohr Siebeck, 2011), 3–31.

5.   The concept of participation is, of course, a central idea to Platonic thought and there is little question that the patristic writers absorbed the concept and its language for Christian theological use, believing it to be consonant with Scripture in important ways. See, for example, M. A. Smalbrugge, 'Augustine and deification. A neoplatonic way of thinking.' *Studia Patristica, LXXV*, no. 1 (2017): 103–108; C. J. De Vogel, 'Platonism and Christianity: A Mere Antagonism or a Profound Common Ground?' *Vigiliae Christianae* 39, no. 1 (1985): 1-62; John D. Turner, *Sethian Gnosticism and the Platonic Tradition* (Bibliothèque Copte de Nag Hammadi, Québec: Presses de l'Université Laval; Louvain-Paris: Éditions Peeters, 2001).

but it is coming to share in God's life as His beloved *adopted* sons and daughters in the *true and eternal* Son.

This life-in-God picture of salvation is directly linked to Christ's life as one of us in the incarnation. God the Son became creaturely flesh and participated in humanity without ceasing to be who and what He is: His true deity was not lost or diluted in some way by becoming man. Our salvation is the mirror image of His journey downwards. We sinful and corrupted humans are elevated to share in God's life and nature without ceasing to be what we are as creatures and as non-divine.[6] The logic is that the Son chose to step into the creation, sharing in the darkness and death of humanity (especially on the cross), so that we could step into the life, relationship, and glory He enjoys with His Father in the Spirit. This is the impassioned desire of Jesus in the prayers He makes to His Father on the night of His crucifixion (John 17:21, 23, 26; also see John 14:23).

This fully orbed and interconnected picture of incarnation and salvation was almost universal in the early church.[7] At the heart of this understanding was a story of salvation that Irenaeus had called 'recapitulation'. He had seen salvation as a three-act drama of creation, fall, and redemption, in which humanity was first created for union with God, but falls in Adam, and is then restored to glorified union with God in Christ. He had drawn upon Ephesians 1:10 – that the Father's plan for the fullness of time is 'to *unite* all things' in Christ. The Greek here means to 'sum-up' or, literally, 're-head' and the Latin for 'head'

---

6. Kenneth Paul Wesche, 'Eastern Orthodox Spirituality: Union with God in *Theosis*' in *Theology Today* 56 (1) (1999), 30.

7. It has sometimes been characterised as an exclusive preoccupation of the East but, in the last few decades, there has been a recognition that the Western fathers also saw the Christian life this way too. See, for example, David Meconi, *The One Christ: St Augustine's Theology of Deification* (Washington DC: Catholic University of America Press, 2013); Norman Russell, 'A Common Christian Tradition: Deification in the Greek and Latin Fathers' in Jared Ortiz (ed.) *Deification in the Latin Patristic Tradition* (Washington DC: Catholic University of America Press, 2019), 272–294.

is *caput*, hence 'recapitulation'. Humanity had been ruined by its father and family head, Adam, but was glorified in its new Head, Jesus Christ (Rom 5:12-21, Col 1:18). The whole drama is centred on Christ, the eternal Word. He stepped into Adam's race to save us from the inside by undoing all that Adam had done. While Adam had gone to a tree in Eden and plunged humanity into sin, condemnation, and death, our new Head, Christ, went to the tree outside Jerusalem's city wall and bought for us righteousness, justification, and life. He became one of us in order to bestow on us His own natural fellowship with the Father.[8]

This understanding of salvation preserves a vital biblical truth. The great benefit of the Christian life is not that we receive a selection of blessings from God, but that we come to share with God the Son in things that are truly only His - indeed, *everything* that is truly His. The greatest early church theologians were crystal clear on this and guarded it like treasure. Any account of salvation that offered less than sonship in the Son, life in the one who is Life, and heart-to-heart communion with God the Father by the Spirit could not support the riches of the Scriptural promises to Christians.

A Minority Report

Against this broad consensus in the early church stood three rather isolated figures: Diodore, Theodore, and Nestorius. Their understanding of salvation - as well as the history of redemption - was entirely different from that handed down from Irenaeus.[9] Their unique two-Son Christology was entirely linked to a unique

---

8. Irenaeus says, 'For it was incumbent upon the Mediator between God and men, by His relationship to both, to bring both to friendship and concord, and present man to God, while He revealed God to man. For, in what way could we be partaken of the adoption of sons, unless we had received from Him through the Son that fellowship which refers to Himself, unless His Word, having been made flesh, had entered into communion with us?' (Irenaeus, *Against Heresies*, III.18.7.)

9. See A. Von Harnack, *History of Dogma*, Theological Translation Library [Trans. W. M'Gilchrist] (London: Williams and Norgate, 1889-9); vol. III, 201.

and contentious soteriology, and it is perhaps best exemplified by Theodore.

For Theodore, the goal of salvation was not so much the believer's fellowship with God, but their attainment of sinlessness and immortality in the life of the age to come.[10] It is something more akin to a vision of personal moral transformation received in heaven than it is to being brought to share in the life of the triune God. Donald Fairbairn has written that Theodore's version of the story of salvation is essentially a 'two-act scheme', in which humanity progresses from one *katastasis* ('age' or 'dispensation') into another. The first age is humanity's natural, created state and, unlike in Irenaeus' thought where the first 'act' was humanity's good creation, Theodore's first age is defined by mutability, corruption, and sin. Irenaeus' second act whereby humanity falls from grace by sinning in Eden is totally missing or conflated with the first: we are characterised by sin and death *in our very beginnings*. Human mortality and suffering, for Theodore, are not the result of sin and a fall, but simply the natural outworking of our mutability and creatureliness in contrast to our immutable and perfect Creator.[11] In other words, Theodore did not hold either to a truly good original creation of humanity nor to an historical fall of Adam in the garden (both key convictions for Irenaeus in his fight against the Gnostics). To be human, for Theodore, is to be imperfect and the task set before us is to make our ascent to the second age of perfection.

Here, Theodore's theology begins to resonate with a theological debate that was rumbling in the West of the empire. Pelagius, a British monk living in Rome, had popularised the idea that each person was responsible for their own sin and their own salvation. Frustrated by nominal Christianity and hypocrisy,

---

10. See Daniel Keating, *Appropriation*, 49. Keating also highlights Norris' 1963 account of Theodore's avoidance of deification.

11. This briefly summarises the excellent section in Fairbairn, *Grace and Christology*, 28–51.

he felt that the concept of 'original sin' made Christians lazy and irresponsible. To say that sin and death came through Adam's fall and that our sinfulness was a result of our inherited nature seemed like an excuse to avoid the moral teaching of Scripture. So, Pelagius preached a 'gospel' that the human problem is that we willingly *copy* Adam in his sin, and that we must learn to *copy* Christ in His blameless life instead. This, he argued, was obviously the point of the law and all God's commands to be holy. Christians simply needed to fire up their willpower and start to take responsibility for their lives and actions. His great opponent (and the man who blew his arguments out of the water) was the mighty Augustine. Augustine argued that Pelagius misunderstood both humanity *and* God, and finally destroyed the gospel by placing our salvation in our own helpless hands.[12] In all his zeal, Pelagius had thrown out the fall, the headship of Adam over humanity, and therefore the gracious salvation that Christ brought *by being the last Adam* (1 Cor 15:45). He was left with a message of self-salvation by individual willpower and effort; the textbook example of salvation by works.

One of Augustine's allies, Marius Mercator, believed that the source of Pelagian teaching was none other than Theodore of Mopsuestia.[13] He may have been correct, for, writing against another anti-Pelagian, Jerome, Theodore does make some jaw-dropping claims that place him very close indeed to Pelagius. He 'makes light of the first sin' in Genesis 3 and 'mocks those who imagine that God flew into a fury over it, and pronounced a universal sentence of sin and death' for that would have

---

12. For more on Pelagius and Augustine on sin and salvation, see Michael Reeves, *Introducing Major Theologians*; then also Peter Brown, *Augustine of Hippo: A Biography* (Berkely: University of California Press, 2000); Pier Franco Beatrice, *The Transmission of Sin. Augustine and the Pre-Augustinian Sources.* Trans. Adam Kamesar (Oxford: Oxford University Press, 2013).

13. Marius Mercator, *Commonitorium, prologus* 3, 1 (ACO I, 5: 5).

been, he believed, the height of injustice.[14] Since some saints were counted righteous in the Old Testament, he reasoned, it surely follows that there is no such thing as 'original sin': nobody was sinful because of Adam, but only through their own choices and actions. The existence of righteous people proves it! Indeed, Theodore maintained that Adam and Eve were created physically mortal but with the potential to achieve immortality in the second age, should they have remained obedient to God.

It is possible to see a sliver of difference between Pelagius and Theodore. Theodore did have a theology of grace in salvation, which seemed absent from Pelagius' outlook. Before we breathe a sigh of relief, though, and clap Theodore on the back, we must understand what he means by 'grace'. Grace is, in Theodore's view, God's way of assisting the graduation of humans into the second age from the first – a divine empowering to make the journey from corruption to incorruption, when sin will finally be removed. It is like a performance battery inserted for those who will co-operate. Indeed, Fairbairn says that, in Theodore's thought, grace is 'a special activity of God... in the lives of those people who are worthy, those who strive to please him.'[15] This version of grace is God's aid for those who will work hard enough: God 'helping those who help themselves'.

What then is the role of Jesus Christ in this Theodoran story of salvation? In Theodore's mind, the 'assumed man' Jesus is the 'uniquely graced' person; the exemplar and model of making use of this assistance. The presence and influence of the Word on Jesus of Nazareth meant that Jesus lived a morally upright life and was freed from corruption and death. He becomes *the* test case and prototype of ascent to the second age. He can function for us in this way since,

---

14.   Elizabeth. A. Clark, *The Origenist Controversy: The Cultural Construction of an Early Christian Debate* (Princeton: Princeton University Press 1992), 206. Clark is dealing with Theodore's *Liber contra Hieronymum* 3; 5.

15.   Fairbairn, *Grace and Christology*, 37.

The man Jesus is similar to all other men, differing from natural men in nothing except that he [the Word] has given him grace.[16]

Likewise, Nestorius wrote that, while Jesus lived in world of temptation, pain, and vexation, he bound himself to the will of God and 'comported himself valiantly', living 'not for himself but for him whose *prosopon* he was' (the Word).[17] Remember, for Theodore and Nestorius, 'Jesus' and 'the Word' are not completely identical. The 'assumed man' is precisely one of us, and what distinguishes him from us is not that he is God's eternal Son in flesh, but only that he has been specially empowered *by* the Word. In fact, the man Jesus was chosen to be such a trailblazer or forerunner for humanity only because God foreknew that he would use the grace of the Word well in his own life, cooperating and entering into a 'partnership' with Him. Fairbairn summarises:

> For Theodore, grace does not consist of God's giving himself to humanity directly. Mankind does not participate by grace in God's own character or his divine life, and Theodore's writings contain essentially no evidence of an idea of deification. Furthermore, Theodore does not place much emphasis on grace as God's giving his fellowship to humanity... Instead, Theodore's focus is on the movement from a lower to a higher *human* existence, not from a human to a *divine* existence or from a state of alienation from God to one of fellowship with him. For Theodore, the immortality and corruption that will characterize the second age are not so much qualities of divine life that we will share, as they are characteristics of a perfected human life, products of free human obedience to God. As a result, he focuses on our partnership with the assumed man who has ascended to the second age, not on our association with God through the assumed man.[18]

---

16. Theodore, *De Incar.* 2.291.

17. *Book of Heracleides*, 1.1.70, 64.

18. *Grace and Christology*, 51–52.

God is not personally involved in the believer's salvation. He gives grace and assistance from afar, as exemplified in the life of Jesus the 'assumed man', but Theodore nowhere recognises God as directly present in union and communion with Christians. In fact, says Fairbairn, Theodore's soteriology finally 'does not demand a direct personal presence of God in the world' at all.[19] His understanding of the person of Christ, grace, and salvation unite in a distinctively human-centred way: optimistic about humanity's ability to ascend, with assistance from divine grace and the example of Jesus. This, combined with his writings during the Pelagian controversy and his documented friendship with Pelagian bishops exiled from the West have earned him the title 'Pelagius before Pelagius.'[20] These connections were not lost on the Western delegates at the Council of Ephesus as they came to examine Nestorius.

Charles Gore, a theologian and bishop in the Church of England during nineteenth century once made a telling remark tying together the Christology and soteriology we have seen here: 'The Nestorian Christ is the fitting saviour of the Pelagian man.'[21] Gore could see that a Christ who was not God the Son in human flesh could not offer anything more to humanity than a moral example to be followed. He could only be an exceptional one from among us and could lead us no further than He Himself could go: to ethical perfection by our co-operation with God. Theodore and Nestorius were not able to see salvation as anything better or richer than this because their Christ was simply not *able* to give anything more. Again, they fell into exactly the same trap as the Arians of generations before. The

---

19. *Grace and Christology*, 40–41.

20. See McGuckin, *The Christological Controversy*, 34–36. Henry Wace recounts that, in 418, Theodore received Pelagian refugees exiled from the West. After giving them shelter for four years, he wrote *Against the Defenders of Original Sin*, directed against Augustine (though addressed to Jerome). Henry Wace, *Dictionary of Christian Biography and Literature* (Boston: Little, Brown and Company, 1911), 967.

21. Charles Gore, 'Our Lord's Human Example', *Church Quarterly Review* 16 (1883): 298.

Arians had imagined a Son who was not of the same being as Father, but who was merely a creature (however highly exalted). Because He was not the eternal, consubstantial Son, He could not offer any sonship: it was not His to give. Cyril saw what Athanasius had seen before him: a defective Jesus, whether that of Arius or Nestorius, would result in a sub-biblical salvation. A Jesus who had to pull Himself together, resist temptation, and 'comport himself valiantly' through divine help in order to make His own ascent to eternal life, can only offer His followers the same arrangement.

It took Cyril's dogged insistence on the old understanding of salvation to protect the church from such pitiful fare. He saw that only a unitive Christology that saw God and humanity together in the *incarnation* could get God and humanity together in *salvation*. Only one Lord Jesus Christ, truly divine and truly human, could grant to believers what Scripture actually promised: adoption to sonship and fellowship with God forever.

'The Magnitude of His Grace'

From long before the Nestorian controversy, Cyril had written with clarity and depth on salvation as communion with God.[22] The Christology he articulated during the conflict with Nestorius was nothing more than the Christology he believed was required to guarantee that. He understood himself to be doing nothing more than upholding Nicene Christianity and defending a Scriptural view of salvation.

Cyril's pre-controversy writings see the incarnation – and the atonement – as the beginning of a beautiful exchange in which Christ took to Himself the sin, corruption, and death of humanity, so that He might bestow upon us His own righteousness and life. He states in the *Commentary on John*:

> The Lamb is to become the second Adam, not from earth but from heaven, and to become the source of all good for human

---

22. See Keating, *Appropriation of Divine Life*, 20-205; and Blackwell, *Christosis*, 71-98.

nature, the deliverance from imported corruption, the bestower of eternal life, the basis for transformation into God... For one lamb "died for all", rescuing the entire flock on earth for God the Father... the Father gave his Son as a ransom for us, once for all, since all are in him, and he is greater than all. One died for all that all may live in him. Death swallowed up the Lamb for all and vomited forth all in him and with him since we were all in Christ who died and was raised for us and on our behalf.[23]

On Isaiah 53, Cyril is equally clear about the nature of the Atonement. He writes that Christ did not suffer for his own sins, 'but He was stricken because of our transgressions'. This punishment had been due to fall on sinners, but 'so that they might cease warring with God, [it] descended upon Him... God delivered Him up because of our sins so that He might release us from the penalty.' This is quoted by J. N. D. Kelly who goes so far as to say that Cyril's 'guiding idea' was that of penal substitution: the Son bearing our sin's penalty as a substitute.[24] Perhaps it is more accurate to say that, for Cyril, Christ is both representative and substitute, or both Priest and Sacrificial Lamb. By uniting himself to us in the incarnation, He is able to unite us to Himself in His death, at once dying *for* us and *with us in Him* – and then bringing us to new life in His resurrection (Rom 6:5; Gal 2:20). Having stood in our place in the incarnation and passion, Christ invites us to stand in His place in salvation.

These early writings are full of the theme of deification and his understanding is very much in line with that of Irenaeus and Athanasius before him. His commentary on John abounds with quotable sections on the nature of salvation. This from John 1:12-13 is a good example:

The Son, by his authority, gives what belongs to him alone by nature and sets it forth as a common possession... We became participants in him through the Spirit... the natural Son gave

---

23. *Jo.* 1:29.

24. J. N. D. Kelly, *Early Christian Doctrines* (London: Adam & Charles Black, 1977), 398.

them power to become children of God, thereby introducing the idea of adoption and grace. Then he goes on without danger to say, "They were born of God." This is to show the magnitude of his grace toward them since he gathers, as it were, what is alien to God the Father into a natural kinship and raises what is servile to lordly nobility because of his fervent love toward it.[25]

The emphasis is on the wonder of grace that means believers may call themselves children of God, all on account of the Son sharing what is His. We who are alien to God the Father (Eph 2:19; Col 1:21) are brought to belong to Him, and we who are low are lifted up to share in His dignity. Again, note the emphasis that only a Christ who is naturally and truly the Son of God can have the authority to bestow such loving adoption.

Commenting on John 14:16–17, Cyril pinpoints the indwelling of the Holy Spirit as the way in which we are made 'partakers of the divine nature'. Since the Spirit, like the Son, is 'of the substance of the Father' and we receive Him, then, 'he becomes a certain quality, so to speak, of the divine nature in us. He dwells in the saints and remains with them forever'. More, the Spirit is the one who will 'sanctify them and make them performers of all good works. He will free them from the shame of slavery that goes with the human condition and will clothe them with the honor of adoption.'[26]

When Cyril comes to write on John 14:20, he is constantly apologising for his inadequacy for the subject and his for discussion being 'more involved than necessary'. But, 'emboldened by the torch of the Spirit' and 'incited by the fervor of love to see and to speak (though within limits)',[27] he has a go. And we can be grateful he did, for the following passage on the incarnation is pure gold and worth quoting at length.

---

25. *Jo.* 1:12–13.

26. *Jo.* 14:16–17. Cyril cross-references Galatians 4:6 here.

27. *Jo.* 14:20.

There was no other way for humanity, being of a perishable nature, to escape death except to be returned to that original grace and to participate once again in God, who holds all things in existence and who gives life through the Son in the Spirit. So he came to share in flesh and blood, that is, he became a human being, even though the only begotten Word of the Father is life by nature and is begotten of him who is life by nature, that is, God the Father. He did this so that by ineffably and indescribably uniting himself to the flesh that was perishing (at least as far as its own nature is concerned) as only he knew how to do, he might raise it to his own life and make it a partaker of God the Father through himself. He is the "mediator between God and humanity," as it is written. As God and from God, he is naturally joined to God the Father. And as a human being, he is joined to humanity, having the Father in himself and himself being in the Father. He is the imprint and radiance of his hypostasis, not distinct from the essence of which he is the imprint and from which he proceeds as radiance, but being in it and having it in him. And he likewise has us in himself in that he bore our nature, and our body is called the body of the Word. "The Word became flesh," as John says. He bore our nature and thus fashioned it in conformity with his life. And he himself is in us, since we have all become partakers in him, and we have him in ourselves through the Spirit. Therefore, we have become partakers of the divine nature and we are called children, since we have the Father himself in us through the Son.

It is a classic passage which lays out Cyril's incarnationally-driven theology of salvation beautifully. As we saw in the last chapter, if it were not the Son suffering on the cross, then it is not God who came down to save us from our sin and death, but a creature. There is 'no other way' for our escape from death except that the Word, who is Life Himself, took our 'perishing' nature through death and raised it up with Him. We are brought to participate in His own eternal life with the Father and the Holy Spirit.

Eagle-eyed readers may spot something a little unusual here, though. Cyril speaks about believers being '*returned* to that original grace' in Christ and participating '*again*' in God. Is he picturing our salvation in Christ as a simple reset button that returns us to the position of Adam in Eden – and perhaps able to fall again? Has Cyril invented his own two-act drama of salvation where the result of salvation is no different to the original creation? No. Certainly, Cyril has a strikingly high view of our created state, in stark contrast to Theodore. He speaks about the creation of humanity in a way that very closely mirrors the way he speaks about salvation. In Genesis 2:7, when God breathed the breath of life into Adam's nostrils, Cyril calls this breath 'the Spirit of the Son' and says that God is making man 'a partaker of his own nature' at that moment in order to keep him from passing into nonexistence.[28] He says that, after the fall, therefore, 'God the Father in Christ wanted to *return* human nature to its original condition and undertook to do so.'[29] It seems that, in speaking this way, Cyril is carefully guarding against Theodore's idea that humanity is elevated or advanced by divine assistance. It was vital to see salvation not as a kind of *promotion* earned by effort, but a *restoration* after a fall, granted by pure grace.

Nevertheless, Cyril is not imagining that salvation as a crude u-turn which only leaves believers back at square one and facing the same old danger. In fact, Cyril understood the believer's position in Christ to be a grace *beyond* the grace of creation. Speaking about our adoption in John 1:12, Cyril seems to put these two ideas together. He writes that we 'recover the ancient beauty of our nature' in salvation, *returning* to the likeness and image of God, but we are also 'refashioned in relation to the divine nature' so that 'we will *be superior to the evils that befell us*

---

28. *Jo.* 14:20. Cf. Daniel Keating's chapter in Weinandy and Keating (eds.) *The Theology of St Cyril of Alexandria* (London: T&T Clark, 2003), 149–185.

29. *Jo.* 14:20 (emphasis mine). Cyril's commentary on John 20:22 picks up the same theme, as the risen Christ breathes the Spirit on the gathered disciples as a sign of renewal.

because of transgression. Therefore, we *rise up to an honor above our nature because of Christ'* and 'enjoy the good that comes by grace rather than the honors that come by nature.'[30] Cyril comments in *Festal Letter* 16, delivered in 428:

> God the Father then sent the Son himself down to us of necessity when we had acted miserably, to bring our condition to an *incomparably better state than of old* and to save those on earth, once sin had been removed, that is, and death, which had sprouted through it, been destroyed, root and all, and in addition the devil's tyranny itself been done away with.[31]

Rather than seeing salvation as a return to 'factory settings' on humanity, Cyril sees that adoption in the Son means a depth of participation in God's life that exceeds even the God-given natural life we'd begun with. Now, the very possibility of sin, death, and corruption are done away with by Christ. His incarnation is an irreversible and matchless union of Himself to humanity, and a union of humanity to Himself. He has taken our humanity with its sin and judgement to death and brought it back victorious into incorruptible life. This not only wins our freedom but brings to us what Adam did not begin with: an unassailable, eternal security.

Loved by the Father in the Son

Cyril's theology of salvation is saturated with the language of grace from the beginning, but Fairbairn writes that Cyril fine-tuned his understanding of grace because of the Nestorian controversy. Rather than talking about grace in some general sense (as something that God could simply pass to the believer), Cyril increasingly seems to identify 'grace' as Christ Himself. He wanted to say that the glory of salvation is that God grants *Himself* to humanity through the Son. The reason Cyril insisted

---

30. *Jo.* 1:12 (emphasis mine).

31. John J. O'Keefe, *St Cyril of Alexandria. Festal Letters 13-30* (Washington DC: Catholic University of America Press, 2013), 55 (Festal Letter 16).

on a unitive Christology is precisely that he wanted to protect his conviction that in the incarnation, God was truly giving Himself. Every time he speaks about the flesh that is the Word's *own* flesh, he is making this exact point: God *Himself* has come to us to bring us *to Himself*.[32]

Cyril says that 'those who have been called by faith to adoption and eternal life must learn not only that God is one and true but also that he is a Father.'[33] God is, above all things, Father to the Son and then, by extension, Father to those who are in the Son. In John 17:23, Jesus prays that believers would know 'that you have sent me and have loved them even as you have loved me.' Cyril makes the observation that the Father begins to relate to the Son in a new way in the incarnation: 'we see him who was beloved for ages now starting to be loved when he became human'. But, says Cyril, this was not something He 'received for himself' for 'he was always and forever loved'. Rather, 'he received this love from the Father when he became human *in order to bestow the Father's love on us*.'[34] He says that just as we will be conformed to Christ's resurrection and glory, so also, we are conformed to His beloved-ness,

> as we yield to the victory of the Only Begotten in all things and justly marvel at the incomparable mercy of the divine nature toward us, which graces those whom he has made with what belongs to him and share with his creatures what belongs to himself alone.[35]

Writing about the same idea in John 17:26, Cyril says,

> Those who are enabled to know God the Father by pure contemplation and who are accurately taught the meaning of the mystery of Christ will surely and without doubt have the

---

32. See Fairbairn, *Grace and Christology*, 105–132.

33. *Jo.* 17:3.

34. *Jo.* 17:23.

35. *Jo.* 17:23.

love of the Father, just as the Son does. The Father loves his Son with a perfect love, and Christ himself dwells in those who know him (through the Holy Spirit) and unites them in a spiritual kinship with God the Father through himself, as they are pregnant with an unperverted knowledge of God.[36]

This adoption by the Father in the Son is sealed in us by the Holy Spirit and is the great honour of our redeemed state that outstrips all that humanity knew in creation.

We ascend to honors above our nature by our likeness to him, for though we are not sons by nature, we are called sons of God, since he cries out in us through his own Spirit, "Abba! Father!"... He says that God is his Father and our God, and both statements are true. By nature and in truth the God of all is the Father of Christ. When it comes to us, however, he is not our Father by nature, but rather our God, since he is creator and Lord. But since the Son has mixed himself with us, in a manner of speaking, he grants to our nature the honor that properly and strictly speaking belongs to him when he refers to his own Father as our common Father.'[37]

Fairbairn puts it this way: 'God does not simply grant us *a* relationship with himself, or *some kind* of fellowship with himself. Instead, he grants us to share by grace in *the very same* fellowship that the persons of the trinity share by nature.'[38] You can imagine the frantic speed of Cyril's pen as he overflows with excitement at the thought:

We are loved as sons in the likeness of him who is truly Son by nature (...) What language could reveal to us how great a blessing it is to be with Christ? We will have unspeakable joy

---

36. *Jo.* 17:26.

37. *Jo.* 20:17. See also Oration 4 of the Hebrews commentary, which dwells on the work of the Son and Spirit in adoption.

38. Fairbairn, *The One Person*, 94-6.

(...) What perfection of invincible joy could they lack whose inheritance is to be with Christ who is Lord of all?[39]

Grace and Faith

Cyril's constant refrain when talking about grace and salvation is that all the blessings of salvation are not ours naturally, and so come to us from outside ourselves. This means that God, rather than us, is the one with power to grant such blessings in the first place – and that it is God's love and grace, rather than our efforts, that sustain and enliven us in the Christian life. God alone is 'the supplier and matchmaker' of the blessing of eternal life.[40] In many ways, Cyril's understanding of salvation anticipates the sixteenth century reformers by emphasising that only God's grace – received by faith – can save. On Romans 3:27, Cyril writes:

> Therefore, he says that boasting is excluded, that is, it is cast out and carried away, since it has no place among us. On what grounds is it excluded? [On the grounds that] we have been made rich by the passing over of previous sins (Rom 3:25), having been justified as a gift by mercy and grace in Christ.[41]

Considering Romans 4:2, which denies that Abraham was justified by works, Cyril deals with the objection that James contradicts Paul in James 2:21. There, Abraham is said to be 'justified' by his offering up of Isaac on the altar (in Genesis 22). Cyril sees no contradiction. Abraham, he says, was 'justified before God' by believing the promise of a son made to him back in Genesis 12, while the later episode was 'a training exercise

---

39. *Jo.* 17:24.

40. *Jo.* 17:3.

41. This is Donald Fairbairn's own translation of Cyril's commentary on the passage, taken from a brilliant article that is well worth reading. In it, Fairbairn defends the idea that Cyril is the greatest patristic exponent of the 'evangelical doctrine of justification by grace'. Donald Fairbairn, 'Justification in St. Cyril of Alexandria,' *Participatio: The Journal of the T.F. Torrance Theological Fellowship* 4, no. 8 (2013): 136.

for the righteous man' and 'a clear proof of the firmness of his faith', which, he says, is the simple point of James 2:22.[42] Indeed, elsewhere, he writes that 'the blessed Abraham himself... who was once enslaved to sin and was set free through faith alone in Christ... Nor did he bestow freedom on himself; he received it from another, namely from Christ himself, who justifies.'[43] For Cyril, the Christian's righteousness before God is nothing other than *Christ's own righteousness*, given from outside us and received by faith as the believer comes to participate in Christ.[44]

Cyril's vision of the Christian life is of continued communion with Christ. Since, in the incarnation, God the Son came to share in our humanity, the Christian life is a reciprocal participation in Him. For Cyril, we share in Christ *spiritually* since He comes to dwell in us by the Holy Spirit, especially in baptism, and we share in Christ *corporeally* as we receive His body and blood in the Eucharist. The Lord's Supper, which he calls 'the Mystical Blessing' has a significant place in his thought. Christ, the Bread of Life, 'nourishes us to eternal life both by supplying us with the Holy Spirit and by participation in his own flesh'.[45] For Cyril, Holy Communion is a reception of Christ's flesh – flesh that brings spiritual life because it is the Word's own flesh, now physically given to us to share.[46] To receive communion is to receive the life-giving flesh of Jesus into ourselves, enabling and embodying our participation in Him. Cyril did not think that the bread and wine had some 'automatic' effect on the communicant (and they had to be received with faith), neither

42. Cyril, *Commentaries on Romans, 1-2 Corinthians, and Hebrews*, ed. Joel C. Elowsky, trans. David R. Maxwell, Ancient Christian Texts (Downers Grove: IVP Academic, 2022), 35–36 (Commentary on Romans 4:2). He has a good point: James directly references Genesis 12 and Genesis 22 in the same chapter.

43. *Jo.* 8:34.

44. See Fairbairn, *Justification in St. Cyril*, 142.

45. *Jo.* 6:35.

46. *Commentary on Hebrews*, 265–277.

was he teaching something akin to later Transubstantiation.[47] Nevertheless, his expectations at the Lord's Table are very high: 'we receive the Son himself into ourselves through the blessing.'[48]

Some readers may find this Eucharistic theology difficult to swallow, but it is worth noting how it could never be articulated by a Nestorian. Cyril is clear in his third letter to Nestorius that going to church to receive the flesh of any normal human being, or even the flesh of a man who had a divine indwelling, would do nobody any good. How, he wonders, could Nestorius see the Supper blessing, sanctifying, and giving life at all, if the flesh of Jesus were not the flesh of the Word Himself? His conviction is that, because of the true and direct participation of God the Son in human flesh, we enjoy true and direct participation in that same flesh in the Eucharist by the Spirit. In this act of communion, we who are naturally corrupt and dying actually receive into our own bodies the blessing of eternal life, since we are sharing in the One who is Life in Himself.[49]

The All-Sufficient Son

Giving voice to the consensus of the early church, Cyril sketched out a picture of grace, salvation, and communion with God in which the one divine-human person of Jesus Christ is totally central. He is the means, the definition, the *place* of humanity's relationship to God. Because it is the Son Himself (clothed in all His humanity, suffering, and death) who is at one time both God

---

47. Daniel Keating, *Appropriation*, 70. Cf. Jo. 6:41, 47.

48. *Jo.* 6:55.

49. My thanks to my student, Pete Gower, whose excellent master's dissertation at Union School of Theology, was a help in writing this section. For more on this theme, see Henry Chadwick, 'Eucharist and Christology in the Nestorian Controversy'. *Journal of Theological Studies* II, no. 2 (1951): 145–164; Ezra Gebremedhin, *Life-giving Blessing: Inquiry into the Eucharistic Doctrine of Cyril of Alexandria* (University of Uppsala, 1977). Matthew Crawford has written that Cyril's conception of participation in Christ extends to believers being 'nourished' by Christ through the Scriptures, too. See chapter five of his *Cyril of Alexandria's Trinitarian Theology of Scripture* (Oxford: Oxford University Press, 2014).

and man, He is able to lay a hand on both (Job 9:33) and be the 'borderland', meeting place, and Mediator. It is His very identity as the God-Man to embody this saving, economic possibility. Cyril writes in the *Scholia on the Incarnation*, that even the name *Jesus* 'has a dynamic significance, in so far as it rises from a *deed*... For scripture says: "He will save his people from their sins."'[50]

Salvation is not only something Jesus does *for* us, but it is truly *in Him*. He is God, come on God's terms to meet humanity in humanity's plight, perfectly uniting the two in Himself. Any 'salvation' wrought by another (even a uniquely graced man assumed by the Word!) would not be the same as the salvation that was wrought by God the Word in human flesh when He saved His people from sin, death, and corruption for renewed communion with God. Where Theodore and Nestorius saw Jesus as a son by grace, Cyril knew that a mere man could no more grant sonship with authority than any other believer. If the baby in the manger and the man on the cross were not God the Word Himself, then there was no salvation, no communion with God, and no way open for God and humanity to meet. The metaphysical convictions underpinning the thought of Diodore, Theodore, and Nestorius meant that there could be no final union of humanity and divinity in any sense at all. Lionel Wickham rightly says:

> It will not do to think of Christ (...) as a very good man (...) or a very inspired man (...) or a very important example of divine grace. It will not do to explain the Incarnation as a union of wills dependent on the essentially transitory and fragile responsiveness of the human subject in Christ. Grace cannot depend on anything, least of all upon the waverings of the best even of human wills. Grace must be unconditional and the Incarnation a binding of the Son of God with man in a union stronger than, because more basic than, any human act

---

50. Cyril, Scholia 3 in McGuckin, *The Christological Controversy*, 296–7 (emphasis mine).

or choice. To divide the one Christ must be to divide man from life and grace.[51]

The bedrock of Cyril's Christological thought, on the other hand, is the gracious salvation that Jesus offers. In Jesus Christ, God is truly among us, and makes Himself available to humanity for our salvation and for eternal fellowship with Himself. By his incarnation and passion, He has taken our sin and death and exchanged it for sonship. For, in the one who is truly and eternally Son, Christians are adopted by the Father of glory. This adoption means that the believer is gathered into the communion which has existed eternally between the Father and the Son; brought to share in the love, glory, righteousness, and joy that has always overflowed from their fellowship in the Spirit. We can account ourselves loved by the Father *just as the Son is*. This is not something we naturally know or enjoy but it *is* Christ's to give, and He has given it freely and forever for all who will come to Him for life.

Only God the Son incarnate could offer such certain salvation and sweet assurance to believers. As Isaac Watts would write centuries later,

Incarnate love
Has seiz'd and holds me in almighty arms:
Here's my salvation, my eternal hope,
Amidst the wreck of worlds and dying nature.
I am the Lord's, and he for ever mine.[52]

51.　Lionel Wickham, *Cyril of Alexandria: Select Letters* (Oxford: Oxford University Press, 1983), xxxv.

52.　Isaac Watts, 'Peace of Conscience, and Prayer for Health', in *The Poems of Watts vol. II. and Yalden*, The British Poets XLVI (Chiswick: C. Witthingham, 1822), 177.

6

CHALCEDON AND BEYOND

In the years after the Council of Ephesus, Cyril's life was perhaps quieter, but he was not able to retire from defending the theology that had animated him for so long. Several theologians and pastors rejected the Formula of Reunion as a sell-out one way or the other and became more entrenched than ever in their opposite views. On the one hand, some of the bishops who had previously supported Nestorius (like Theodoret of Cyrus) now leant instead on Theodore of Mopsuestia and circulated his writings. This greatly aggravated Cyril and his friends who knew that Theodore was the main source of Nestorius' theology. Because of this, much of Cyril's effort in his later years was given to writing against Diodore and Theodore. On the other extreme, men like Dioscorus (who would come to be Cyril's successor in Alexandria) suspected that Cyril, growing old and infirm, had gone soft with the Formula. Surely the rambunctious Cyril of the twelve anathemas would never have come to terms with someone as compromised as John of Antioch or agreed to speak of 'two *physeies*' in Christ! They began to feel they could 'out-Cyril' Cyril himself.

On 27th June 444, Cyril died in Alexandria. We do not know how he died or where he was buried, but he was about 69 years old. He had seen the condemnation of Nestorianism by the church and played his part in its downfall, but he certainly did not die under the impression that everything was settled when it came to Christology. In many ways, it is a shame he could not have lived to see the impact of his theology on the faith of the church in the following seven or so years. He probably would have enjoyed what followed.

The Curious Case of Eutyches

In 448, four years after Cyril's death, a hastily assembled council met in Constantinople to confront the teaching of a monk by the name of Eutyches.[1] He had lived in the city for many years and, because he had steadfastly opposed the teaching of Nestorius in his own back yard, he believed that any talk at all of 'Christ in two natures' was unacceptable. Eutyches believed that two distinct natures *had* come together in the incarnation, but only one *physis* remained once the union had occurred. Christ, he said, was '*out of* two natures', and that the substance (*ousia*) of Christ was properly the divine nature, rather than the human nature.[2] Eutyches' opponents had argued that, if this were so, the humanity of Jesus seemed almost engulfed by the divinity, like a drop of wine might be diffused in the ocean. The council, a relatively small and local affair, quickly condemned Eutyches' teaching for its dissolution of the true humanity of Christ. This conclusion was supported by Pope Leo I of Rome the following year in a letter (Letter 28) to Flavian, the chair of the council. In what is now known as his *Tome*, Leo argued that the one person of Jesus Christ had to be considered *in* two natures after the union since the single divine person joined to himself a humanity that had not existed independently before the union.[3]

---

1.   Price and Gaddis, *Acts of the Council of Chalcedon*, 25-30.

2.   For the minutes of this council, which were read out three years later at Chalcedon, see Price and Gaddis, *Acts of the Council of Chalcedon*, 168ff.

3.   Leo I, "The Tome of St. Leo," in *The Seven Ecumenical Councils*, ed. Philip Schaff and Henry Wace, trans. Henry R. Percival, vol. 14, A Select Library of the Nicene

In Alexandria, Dioscorus was incandescent that Eutyches had been condemned for what he felt was nothing more than Cyril's position (at least the Cyril he had admired before the Formula of Reunion). He believed that Constantinople and Rome were betraying Cyril, Ephesus, and orthodox theology. Dioscorus seems to have skipped over the *theological* point that Cyril had wanted to make and was fixated, rather woodenly, on the terminology alone. Cyril had been willing to bend on the exact use of words like *physis* so long as it was clear that the Son of Mary was the Son of God. His concern had not so much been the precise language used, but the doctrine it revealed. In his zeal, though, Dioscorus gathered a second council in Ephesus in 499, no doubt choosing the location to make a point about continuity with Cyril. He refused to have Leo's *Tome* read out in the council, and ensured that Eutyches was exonerated, Flavian condemned, and Cyril's twelve anathemas affirmed. Leo famously called it the *Latrocinium* or 'Robber Council' and begged the emperor to overturn its decisions. Theodosius was very sympathetic to Dioscorus, though, and upheld the council and all his decisions, in many ways leaving an open wound in the church as tensions rose between east and west. All parties believed they were following Nicaea, Cyril, and Ephesus, but simply would not accept one another.

Leo had only to wait patiently for one year for some resolution. In 450, while he was out riding on his horse, the emperor was thrown from the saddle, breaking his spine. He died shortly afterwards and his successor, Marcian (not to be confused with the earlier heretic, Marcion), quickly agreed to hold a council to break the deadlock in the church. It was set for October 451 in the city of Chalcedon, just across the Bosphorous from Constantinople.

and Post-Nicene Fathers of the Christian Church, Second Series (New York: Charles Scribner's Sons, 1900), 43 (*Letter* 38, VI).

The Council of Chalcedon

The Council of Chalcedon was the church's fourth ecumenical council, attended by around 520 bishops, and lasting just under one month. The gold standard introduction and summary is by Richard Price and it includes an excellent introduction as well as the records of proceedings.[4] The council began with a trial of Dioscorus, who must have been blindsided by the change in his fortunes. His orthodoxy, rather than Leo's or Flavian's, was now under the microscope. The emperor had hoped the council would produce a definitive statement of faith, but the gathered bishops preferred to turn to Cyril's second letter to Nestorius, the Formula of Reunion, and Leo's *Tome*. They saw substantial unity between all these documents and initially resisted the urge to add anything to them. Cyril's writings were treated as the plumbline in the decision making at the council, even being preferred to the Pope's letter, which arguably had moments of slight unclarity about the two natures of Christ. Leo had written, for instance, on the two natures that

> each "form" does the acts which belong to it, in communion with the other; the Word, that is, performing what belongs to the Word, and the flesh carrying out what belongs to the flesh; the one of these shines out in miracles, the other succumbs to injuries.[5]

Could the humanity of Christ be spoken of as 'acting' if it isn't a separate personal subject? Three passages like this in the *Tome* were cross-examined by a sub-committee for any whiff of Nestorianism using the already acclaimed teaching of Cyril and his twelve anathemas. In the end, many of the council fathers agreed that what Leo had written accorded with Cyril, not least because he clearly intended to speak about the single person of Christ in the incarnation. For example, he had written that:

---

4.   Richard Price and Michael Gaddis, *The Acts of the Council of Chalcedon* (3 vols) (Liverpool: Liverpool University Press, 2007).

5.   Leo, *Letter* 28 IV, in Price and Gaddis, *Acts*, 256.

on account of this unity of Person which is to be understood as existing in both the natures, we read, on the one hand, that 'the Son of Man came down from heaven,' inasmuch as the Son of God took flesh from that Virgin of whom he was born; and on the other hand, the Son of God is said to have been crucified and buried, inasmuch as he underwent this, not in his actual Godhead; wherein the Only-begotten is coeternal and consubstantial with the Father, but in the weakness of human nature.[6]

The orthodoxy of Leo's letter was essentially judged and confirmed on the basis of Cyril's key concern. The council fathers declared,

This is the faith of Archbishop Leo. Leo believes accordingly. Leo and Anatolius believe accordingly. We all believe accordingly. As Cyril so we believe. Eternal is the memory of Cyril. As is contained in the letters of Cyril, so we hold. We have believed accordingly, and we believe accordingly. Archbishop Leo thinks, believes and wrote accordingly.[7]

This meant the rejection of both Eutyches (against whom Leo had written his *Tome*) and Dioscorus (who was exiled by the emperor). Thirteen bishops from Egypt, however, refused to accept Leo's *Tome* and believed the council had departed from Cyril, much as Dioscorus himself did. This was an impasse. Everybody wanted to uphold Cyril's central thrust, but there was disagreement about how this was to be done, and whether Leo's letter had done enough. The emperor demanded that, although it was the last thing any of the bishops wanted, some kind of statement of faith must be composed. The 'Chalcedonian Definition' that emerged was not really new. It directly quotes the Creed of Nicaea (325) and the Nicene Creed (381) and is an effort to draw-out the implications of the faith of Nicaea. The

---

6.   Leo, *Letter* 28 IV, in Price and Gaddis, *Acts*, 256-257.

7.   Price and Gaddis, *Acts*, 14.

Definition does this, implementing Cyril's key theological move (about the single person in the incarnation), and affirms these things against Eutychianism. It has a complex task!

> We, then, following the holy Fathers, all with one consent, teach men to confess one and the same Son, our Lord Jesus Christ, the same perfect in Godhead and also perfect in manhood; truly God and truly man, of a reasonable [rational] soul and body; consubstantial [coessential] with us according to the manhood; in all things like unto us, without sin; begotten before all ages of the Father according to the Godhead, and in these latter days, for us and for our salvation, born of the Virgin Mary, the mother of God, according to the Manhood; one and the same Christ, Son, Lord, Only-begotten, to be acknowledged in two natures (*physeis*), inconfusedly, unchangeably, indivisibly, inseparably; the distinction of natures being by no means taken away by the union, but rather the property of each nature being preserved, and concurring in one person (*prosopon*) and one Subsistence (*hypostasis*), not parted or divided into two persons (*prosopa*), but one and the same Son, and only begotten, God the Word, the Lord Jesus Christ, as the prophets from the beginning [have declared] concerning him, and the Lord Jesus Christ himself has taught us, and the Creed of the holy Fathers has handed down to us.[8]

The fathers attempted to rule out *both* Nestorianism and Eutychianism by speaking of two 'natures' (*physeis*) but only one 'person' (*prosopon* and *hypostasis*). It maintains that the two natures cannot be blurred into one new thing or jumbled in any way, but eight times specifies that Jesus is 'the same one' or 'one and the same' as the eternal Word.[9] This single person is both *truly God* and *truly man*.

Some in the east, nevertheless, regarded Chalcedon as a fudge. They continued to prefer Cyril's earlier language in which

---

8.   *Historic Creeds and Confessions*, electronic ed. (Oak Harbor: Lexham Press, 1997).

9.   See Donald Fairbairn and Ryan Reeves, *The Story of Creeds and Confessions*, 101–104.

physis meant something closer to 'person' than 'nature', and so Leo's and Chalcedon's dyophysitism seemed like a surrender to Nestorianism and Nestorius' own terminology. Holding to Cyril's old formula, 'one incarnate *physis* of God the Word', this group came to be known as 'Monophysites'. It is important to note that they were not Monophysite in the sense that Eutyches was, however. By using *physis* in a different way to the Formula of Reunion, the *Tome*, and the Chalcedonian Definition, they were not advocating a single divine-human blended *nature* in Christ; but one *person*. This tradition lives on today in the Oriental Orthodox churches (Coptic, Ethiopian, and others) who would refer to their Christology as 'Miaphysite' to distinguish it from Eutychianism. In the same way, bishops in the Church of the East who had always supported Nestorius rejected the Definition, as they had rejected the Council of Ephesus before it. It was known as the 'Nestorian Church' and regarded Nestorius as a saint, along with Theodore of Mopsuestia.[10] Today, this tradition lives on in the Assyrian Church of the East and the Chaldean Catholic Church.

Getting Chalcedon Right

Understanding the nuances of the Council of Chalcedon has not always been easy – and this has been made much more complex by the old 'two schools' theory that we explored in chapter two. Because of the terminological shift around *physis* and the willingness to speak of 'two natures' in Christ, the Chalcedonian Definition has often been presented in modern Western theology as the ultimate compromise between the 'School of Alexandria' and the 'School of Antioch'. It is sometimes said

---

10. It is worth noting that Nestorian Christianity was the dominant kind in those eastern parts of the Roman Empire which nurtured the early development of Islamic theology. A meeting with a Nestorian monk is said (in both Christian and Islamic traditions) to have been formative for the young Mohammed, and the similarities between the Nestorian and Islamic doctrines of God, Christ, and salvation are not difficult to detect. See Barbara Roggema, *The Legend of Sergius Baḥīrā* (Leiden: Brill, 2009).

that the fathers accepted some language from both 'schools', being willing to take the best from the moderate representatives of both camps while wisely excluding the extremists from each end of the spectrum. While the Alexandrians might tend to 'overemphasise' Christ's divinity and the Antiochenes may 'overemphasise' His humanity, the council sagely tried to hold both in a healthy tension. It is as if, after years of squabbling, the church (especially led by Leo) finally found something like a sensible consensus. R. V. Sellers' influential 1953 book, for example, says that the council

> accepted the *Tome* of Pope Leo as a safeguard against Eutychianism, and the letters of Cyril as a safeguard against Nestorianism; but it also accepted what had been taught positively by the Alexandrians on the unity of Christ's Person, by the Antiochenes on the reality of his two natures, and by the Westerns on both these truths.[11]

This is an inaccurate (not to mention slightly patronising) view of the Chalcedonian Definition. It makes the theological method of the early church look decidedly shaky. It would mean that the 'Alexandrians' being allowed a voice here would include Apollinarius and Eutyches as much as Cyril, and the 'Antiochenes' getting their say would include Diodore and Theodore as much as John of Antioch. Somewhere between them, in a central cluster sit Leo and Flavian. The Definition would appear to be a loose ringfence around that central area, or a centre with a gravitational pull. The trouble is that this view asks us to imagine the early church theologians allowing Eutyches and Diodore a voice in determining their theology, as though finding the exact mid-point between two heresies they wished to condemn could lead to orthodoxy! But no early church theologian believed that achieving the perfect balance

---

11. R. V. Sellers, *The Council of Chalcedon: A Historical and Doctrinal Survey* (London: Society for Promoting Christian Knowledge, 1953), 349.

of two errors could unveil the truth. Neither did they believe they were carving out a compromise between two equally valid and equally weighted perspectives. Despite the discomfort some scholars seem to feel about it, we have to say that Chalcedon came down firmly on the side of an 'Alexandrian' thinker: Cyril. As Price writes, 'it would be a mistake to think of the Chalcedonian fathers as themselves consciously attempting a synthesis between Alexandria and Antioch' because they 'believed they were being loyal to Cyril.'[12]

The overwhelming consensus of the early church was to give no space to either Eutychianism or Nestorianism, and, in trying to defend against a whole range of errors in Christology, the fathers clearly regarded Cyril's theology as their most powerful resource. They did not imagine 'two schools' in an impossible balancing act, nor did they try to identify common ground between those they regarded as heretics: they wanted to stand by the truth of the Nicene Creed as interpreted by Cyril. In fact, they consciously saw their work as a continuation of the councils of Nicaea, Constantinople, and Ephesus and intended their Definition to be understood *in the light of* those historical pronouncements. They considered the Son of Mary to *be* the Son of God. This *one* Son and Lord, Jesus Christ, is eternally *homoousios* with the Father, and it was *the same one* who came down and was incarnate *for us and for our salvation*. As Fairbairn and Reeves say,

> it is *a way* to express the consensus truth that God the Son personally came down and became a man so that he, the Son, could live, die, and be raised as a man for our salvation (...) what is universal about the Chalcedonian Definition is not its word usage, its terminology, or its philosophical tenor. Instead, what is universal is the faith that it proclaims—the faith that the

---

12. Price and Gaddis, *Acts*, 73.

baby born from the Virgin Mary is the same person who has always been the Father's only Son.[13]

In other words, the Chalcedonian Definition upholds *all* that we have seen about Cyril's theology: his Christology, but also his doctrine of God and his soteriology. Chalcedon, building as it did on the patristic theology that preceded it, did not really attempt to settle a battle between 'two schools' over Christological terminology. It set out to safeguard the ancient vision of a God who makes Himself known, offers fellowship with Himself, and invites us into His own life through the incarnation of His Son. It puts Jesus Christ, true God and true man, at the centre of revelation and salvation – even *in* the economy of His flesh; in His suffering and death. It makes Jesus the Son of Mary the focal point of the relationship between God and humanity since He is both divine and human. In Jesus Christ, *God truly touched the world*. The doctrine of divine impassibility, understood rightly, need be no barrier to affirming that the Word personally took human life, suffering, and death to Himself in the incarnation and bridged the gap between Creator and creature, incorruptible and corruptible, immortal and mortal. We humans, in all our sin and sorrow have been pursued by God, united to Him, and brought to share in His divine life by the gracious in-breaking of the Son in the person of Jesus Christ. That is Chalcedonian Christianity.

All Cyril's Christological terminology – from '*Theotokos*' to 'hypostatic union' – and all the energy he expended in defending it was designed to buttress and defend this precise view of salvation and of God. His entire Christology, the engine of Chalcedon, is actually an insistence on a particular view of the relationship between God and humanity. This is modelled and worked out in Jesus Christ. He reveals, enacts, and purchases this relationship so that we may all enjoy it in Him. For Cyril

---

13. Fairbairn and Reeves, *Creeds and Confessions*, 107–108.

and for Chalcedon, what a theologian does with the union (or not!) of divinity and humanity in Christ, they also do with the union (or not!) of divinity and humanity in the Christian life.

Harnack's Mirage

It is worth considering briefly how and why the old 'two schools' theory came into being and spotting some of the results of its dominance. This will help us as we turn to look, finally, at some of the ways Cyril's legacy has shaped – and could still help shape – the Church of today.

We noted in chapter two that the idea of 'two schools' is traceable to John Henry Newman in the nineteenth century. Newman was part of a movement that wanted to combat rising theological liberalism in the Church of England, in part by retrieving patristic theology, with Cyril among his chosen fighters. But it was a liberal theologian, Adolf von Harnack, a generation after Newman, who really took hold of the idea and used it to conjure an illusion for his own ends. Harnack, deeply committed to historical-critical theology, rejected most of the 'dogma' of the Christian tradition as a Greek encroachment upon the pure message of Jesus' gospel. Jesus' focus, he said, was His ethical teaching, while the belief that He was 'divine' was a much later accretion. Dismissing the infallibility of Scripture, miracles, and the supernatural, Harnack famously summarised the Christian message as nothing more than 'the Fatherhood of God and the brotherhood of man.'[14]

When Harnack saw the likes of Diodore, Theodore, and Nestorius, he appreciated their focus on Jesus as a man, their denial of an over-arching Christological narrative in Scripture, and the fact that they eschewed a vision of supernatural

---

14. Adolf von Harnack, *What is Christianity? Lectures Delivered in the University of Berlin during the Winter-Term 1899-1900* (trans. Thomas Bailey Saunders) Second Edition. London: Williams and Norgate, 1908.

deification in favour of Christianity as moral progress.[15] He believed they were closer to the original gospel as he saw it. He recognised that this gaggle of thinkers had largely been left outside the grand tradition that had shaped Nicaea and Chalcedon, so he made every effort to craft an umbrella term, a history, and a pedigree for them in an 'Antiochene School'. He wrote about their thought as a coherent and principled tradition, but was beleaguered and unable to wield any influence, as 'Alexandrian' winners wrote the church's history and codified its doctrine. He explicitly identified himself with that theology, rather than what became known as 'orthodoxy'. He wrote, for example,

> People hated [the theology of Antioch] for the same reason they hate the liberals in the Church in the present day... The Antiochians got the blame of 'denying the divinity of Christ' and of dividing the one Christ in two.[16]

He wrote that this was because, while most of the early church went the way of the philosophising and doctrinaire 'Alexandrians' in a tide of 'traditionalism',[17] the Antiochenes were, all along, the pure exegetes of the early church. He says that, while they did not reject wholesale the 'spiritual' meaning of Scripture which had so fascinated others, they tried to determine it from the 'literal meaning' through 'sound exegesis'. [18] This was 'sober,'[19] 'more rational... less flighty...' and Theodore (the ablest Antiochene, in his view) had a 'natural theology without any transcendentalism',[20] engaging in 'grammatico-historical

---

15. Here, it is interesting to note Cyril's accusation (in Letter 73) that Theodore taught that the apostles did not know that Christ was God, and that the church was built on 'human faith'. (McEnerney, *Letters 51–110*, 76).

16. Harnack, *History of Dogma* vol. IV, 244–5.

17. Harnack, *History of Dogma* vol. III, 152, 207; vol. IV, 139 (fn. 1), 315.

18. Harnack, *History of Dogma* vol. III, 201 (fn. 2).

19. Harnack, *History of Dogma* vol. IV, 345, 347.

20. Harnack, *History of Dogma* vol. IV, 545.

exegesis', which essentially 'followed sound principles'.[21]
Harnack's analysis here is probably the reason most people
associate the 'two schools' – or the debate between Cyril and
Nestorius – with the question of biblical exegesis. It is probably
the reason many evangelicals, upon reading an introductory
level summary of 'Antiochene versus Alexandrian' theology,
instinctively assume the so-called 'Antiochenes' are the good
guys. Yet this misses that Harnack's vantage point is his liberal,
critical theology.

When Harnack begins to describe Antiochene biblical
exegesis, it begins to feel more tricky for evangelicals to get on
board. The 'literal' interpretation of Scripture he applauds in
Antiochene exegesis is their breaking down of the history of
'salvation' into a 'Jewish' narrative in the Old Testament and
a 'Christian' one in the New. The story of people, land, and
historical events in the Hebrew Scriptures is really the property
of the Jewish people and has no inherent connection to Christ.
So, Harnack says,

> the number of directly Messianic passages in the O. T.
> became extraordinarily limited; while, according to pneumatic
> [spiritual] exegesis, everything in the O. T. was in a sense directly
> Messianic, i.e. Christian, the Antiochenes only retained a few
> such passages. The horizon of the O. T. authors was more
> correctly defined. Theodore decidedly disputed the presence of
> anything in the O. T. about the Son of God or the Trinity.[22]

For Harnack, seeing Christian or Messianic meaning in the text
was to 'spiritualise', impose, or back-read Christianity into what
he regarded as being simply Jewish texts. Writers like Theodore,
he believed, gave the text its due and he felt Theodore's approach
was an obvious improvement on the Christologically-driven

---

21. Harnack, *History of Dogma* vol. III, 201.

22. Harnack, *History of Dogma* vol. III, 201 (fn. 2).

Alexandrians'.[23] Nevertheless, he laments that, by the Council of Chalcedon, Antiochene Christology could not triumph over the Alexandrian for it had 'long ago succumbed'. The Antiochene patriarchs' behaviour was 'unspeakably pitiful', and they exhibited 'miserable powerlessness.'[24] If only they had stood their ground, perhaps the true gospel might also have stood against the pollution of 'dogma'! The fact that these men went the way of Arius, being condemned and excommunicated by the church, will have disappointed Harnack.

John Behr writes that 'Antiochene' exegesis appeared 'self-evident' in the nineteenth and twentieth centuries at the zenith of critical theology. He notes that H. B. Swete commended Theodore in 1877 for his 'firm grasp of the grammatical and historical method' and for anticipating 'the most recent conclusions of exegesis'.[25] Like Harnack, Swete clearly identified in Theodore something like the foreshadowing of biblical criticism. There is no doubt that this appropriation of the theology of Theodore and others is quite anachronistic. Harnack calls Theodore's exegetical method 'liberal'[26] but Theodore would not have known the meaning of the word and would not have accepted many of Harnack's conclusions. Still, Harnack felt these thinkers were useful to him and the mirage of a great but unfortunate 'school' was the best way to make them seem palatable and reputable. His efforts resulted in what Behr calls a 'sympathy for all things Antiochene, understood very much in terms of our own twentieth-century prejudices and set in opposition to all things Alexandrian'.[27]

---

23. Harnack, *History of Dogma* vol. III, 201 (fn. 2).

24. Harnack, *History of Dogma* vol. IV, 215.

25. Behr, *Diodore and Theodore*, 35.

26. Harnack, *History of Dogma* vol. IV, 545.

27. Behr, *Diodore and Theodore*, ix.

This has certainly been the case in Western – and especially Protestant – theology for the last two hundred years or so.[28] The beginning of the twentieth century saw a movement to rehabilitate and re-appropriate Nestorius, with the charge led from Germany by Eduard Schwartz and Friedrich Loofs, the latter of whom was influenced by the teaching of Harnack in Leipzig.[29] Loofs' 1905 collection, *Nestoriana*, was influential. The discovery in 1895 of a sixteenth-century copy of *The Bazaar of Heracleides* gave unprecedented access to Nestorius' mature theology first-hand. Meanwhile, Cyril's works were conspicuously absent from Philip Schaff's famous *Library of Nicene and Post-Nicene Fathers* that stretched from 1886–1900.[30] This, perhaps coupled with his poor reputation due to the murder of Hypatia and the easy dismissal of his 'Alexandrian' theology, meant he was unjustly neglected for some time. It has only been as patristics scholars steadily began to undermine the old 'two schools' theory that Cyril's theology has been recognised afresh in the west for its brilliance, and his influence on the Chalcedonian Definition seen for what it is.[31] David R. Maxwell notes that Cyril was often passed over as a biblical interpreter because of the prominent discussion of his Christology, yet his 'mastery of the contents of the Bible' is 'breathtaking.'[32]

28. See the discussion in Mark Edwards, *Aristotle and Early Christian Thought* (London: Routledge, 2019), 132–134.

29. See Claus-Dieter Osthövener, "Zur Gelehrtenfreundschaft zwischen Friedrich Loofs und Adolf von Harnack" in Jörg Ulrich (ed.) Friedrich *Loofs in Halle*, (Berlin: De Gruyter, 2010), 63ff.

30. Gregory K. Hillis, "Introduction," in *St. Cyril of Alexandria: Glaphyra on the Pentateuch*, vol. 1, FC 137 (Washington, DC: Catholic University of America Press, 2018), 3.

31. See, for example, Donald Fairbairn, 'Patristic Exegesis and Theology: The Cart and the Horse', *Westminster Theological Journal* 69 (2007): 2; Norman Russell, *Cyril of Alexandria*, ECF (New York: Routledge, 2000), vii.

32. David R. Maxwell, "Translator's Introduction", *Commentary on John* (Downers Grove: IVP Academic, 2013), xv.

Cyril and Mary

One reason Protestant theologians have sometimes continued to be wary of Cyril is his association with the *Theotokos* title for Mary. With half an eye on later veneration of the saints, evangelicals have sometimes supposed that Nestorius might have been speaking sense when he rejected the title. We have seen that the primary intent of the title was to make a *Christological* point rather than a comment about Mary. However, it is the case that the Council of Ephesus probably contributed to a growing fascination with Mary which went further than the Scriptures themselves do.[33]

Mary has always been an important figure in the Church's theology and imagination. The Mary of the Gospels and Acts is a humble, prayerful, and courageous believer who made her Son her treasure, knowing him to be her Lord and God (Luke 2:19, 51; John 2:5). Her quietly profound faith and obedience, especially in the face of scandal and disgrace, stand as an example to be imitated. Mary's song in Luke 1:46-55, the *Magnificat*, became a fixture in early Christian liturgy as the church adopted Mary's words of praise as part of corporate worship. The early apologists Justin Martyr and Irenaeus saw in Mary a 'New Eve' whose role in the Nativity and life of Jesus functioned as foil to her predecessor. Where Eve had been tempted and failed along with the first Adam, Mary's obedience led to the birth of the Last Adam. This was a theological and doctrinal reflection on Mary's part in the coming of salvation. Yet around this time, and on into the third century, there were the shoots of something more: a *devotional* focus on Mary. This was not found so much in the theological writers of the day or the teaching of the church, but in the popular piety of believers in some places. Books like the second century *Protoevangelium of James* popularised the idea that Mary's own conception, birth, and childhood were miraculous

---

33. See Leonardo De Chirico, *A Christian's Pocket Guide To Mary* (Fearn: Christian Focus, 2017) for an excellent overview.

and that she remained a virgin, even after the birth of Jesus. The *Odes of Solomon*, likely written around the same time, claimed that Mary experienced no pain while giving birth to Christ. Some have wondered whether this was the sneaky introduction of pagan goddess worship in a Christianised form, or a kind of proto-feminism. It was more likely part of a generally increasing interest in the saints and a growing sense of connectedness to them.

What changed at the Council of Ephesus and with the adoption of '*Theotokos*' was the enshrining of a *theology* of Mary, constructed by bishops and formally accepted by the church as a whole. With Cyril and Ephesus, Mary arguably became part of the structure of soteriology, and *Theotokos* more than a simple slogan in the Christological controversy. It seems very likely that Cyril and the council fathers leant on the popular Marian spirituality of the day in order to secure their case against Nestorius. Many Christians felt a kind of affection for Mary and it would not have been difficult to arouse their displeasure with Nestorius. This was politically clever, but almost certainly not helpful since popular Mariology developed beyond the council into the practice of praying to Mary and veneration of her, even, in some ways, over and above other saints.[34]

During the Council of Ephesus, Cyril apparently preached a sermon defending the use of *Theotokos* against Nestorius. It makes for striking reading.

> I salute you, O Mary, *Theotokos*: through you... the true light came into the world, our Lord Jesus Christ... Through you, the beauty of the Resurrection flowered, and its brilliance shone out... Through you, every faithful soul achieves salvation... Hail, Mary, you are the most precious creature in the whole world;

---

34. As well as Leonardo De Chirico's book, mentioned above, see Stephen J. Shoemaker, *Mary in Early Christian Faith and Devotion* (New Haven: Yale, 2016) and Luigi Gambero, *Mary and the Fathers of the Church: The Blessed Virgin Mary in Patristic Thought* (San Francisco: Ignatius Press, 1999). These give a good overview of the emergence of devotion to Mary and the theology that grew with it.

hail, Mary, uncorrupt dove; hail, Mary, inextinguishable lamp;
for from you was born the Sun of justice.[35]

Roman Catholic theologian, Luigi Gambero enthuses that this
homily inaugurated a style of preaching in which 'the preacher
would teach Marian truths by means of praises addressed to the
Blessed Virgin'.[36] Certainly it reads like a prayer of thanksgiving
to Mary as though our salvation in Jesus were *her* gift. There
is a debate over whether the work is actually Cyril's, and the
discussion tends to revolve around the possible date of the
delivery of the sermon and whether Cyril could realistically have
been present in the church to preach it.[37] Added to all this, we
know that other versions of this homily were found; later forms,
reworked and embellished in ways that are clearly not Cyril's
work.[38] But do the *contents* of the homily match Cyril's theology
as a whole? At no time in any of his writings does Cyril encourage
the invocation of Mary in prayer.[39] The festal letters of his early
episcopate include only a single passing reference to Mary, and it
is only as the Nestorian controversy begins that she is mentioned
more often, including being referred to as '*Theotokos*'. It would
be hard to make a case that Mary was a preoccupation of
Cyril's pastoral ministry and spirituality. Certainly, he nowhere
positions Mary a mediator of salvation, able to provide her Son
to other humans by means of her own perfection or holiness in

---

35. Homily IV, PG 77, quoted in Gambero, *Mary of the Fathers of the Church*, 243–245.

36. Gambero, *Mary of the Fathers of the Church*, 241.

37. E. Schwartz (ACO I, 1, 2, p. 102; I, 1, 4, p. XXV; I, 1, 8, p. 12) says it is not Cyril's,
    while its authenticity is defended by R. Caro, 'La Homiletica Mariana Griega en
    El Siglo V: II: Parte Primera: Homilias de Dudosa Autenticidad', *Marian Library
    Studies* vol. 4, article 4 (1972), 269–344, and M. Santer, 'The Authorship and
    Occasion of Cyril of Alexandria's Sermon on the Virgin (Hom. Div. iv),' *Studia
    Patristica* 12 (1975): 144-50.

38. See Susan Wessel, *Cyril of Alexandria and the Nestorian Controversy: The Making of a
    Saint and a Heretic* (Oxford: Oxford University Press, 2004), 233.

39. Richard Price, 'The Virgin as Theotokos at Ephesus (AD 431) and Earlier' in Chris
    Maunder (ed.) *The Oxford Handbook of Mary* (Oxford: Oxford University Press,
    2019), 75.

some way. His picture of Mary is actually rather more down-to-earth. When he writes about Mary's tears at the foot of the cross, he says that the 'unexpected suffering that happened to the Lord probably caused even the Lord's mother to stumble'. [40] He imagines that she may have inwardly doubted His divinity and the truth of His words in His teaching. The horror of Christ's suffering was Simeon's sword (Luke 2:35) that 'would divide the woman's mind into strange thoughts' that were not fitting.[41] It may not to be too much to wonder if the texts of this sermon have only a tenuous connection to him.

Nevertheless, whether Cyril intended it or not, the theological move at Ephesus was the open door for later Marian theology to enter. As Leonardo De Chirico writes,

> The 'motherhood' of Mary obtained dogmatic affirmation. It became the entry point for extending the motherhood of Mary to other areas, such as mother of the church, or the human race, and the precedent for the modern Marian dogmas of her immaculate conception (1854) and bodily assumption (1950).[42]

Christology After Chalcedon

As with the Council of Ephesus, after Chalcedon, the church was not able to conclude its discussions about Christology. The fifth and sixth ecumenical councils were dedicated to Christological concerns. They revolved around finding greater clarity on the concepts of *person* and *nature* which had been so central in the debates from Ephesus onwards. It was generally understood that *persons* were real, acting subjects who could do things, while *natures* were the way in which things like persons were manifested. It would be human nature to be hungry, but only human persons could perform the action of eating. While

---

40. *Jo.* 19:25.

41. *Jo.* 19:25.

42. Leonardo De Chirico, *A Christian's Pocket Guide to Mary* (Fearn: Christian Focus Publications, 2017), 27–28.

mortality is not a property of the divine nature, a person with a human nature *can* die, according to that nature. This sort of logic is found in Cyril and Chalcedon when they speak of *one person* known *in two natures* and it formed the bedrock of the discussions that followed.

Chalcedon had assumed that Christ's human nature was *anhypostatic*, that is, it did not have its own *person*. The Son took on a non-personal humanity, with no separate *person* called Jesus. This negative term clearly corrected the Nestorian error of imagining two personal sons in a kind of relationship to one another, but it did risk the idea that the Son had simply taken to Himself a lump of flesh. What about Christ's human individuality? Did He enjoy dancing or not? Did He like or dislike olives? Was He an introvert or an extrovert? What about His mind and will? At the Second Council of Constantinople (553), a second term was adopted (probably borrowed from Leontius of Jerusalem, 485–543) to serve as the other, positive side of the coin. It was said that, while the human nature was *anhypostatic*, it was not devoid of a person. It was *enhypostatic*, that is, it was 'in-personed' or given its *hypostasis* and personhood by God the Son. In this way, the human nature was *made* personal in the incarnation. Just as Cyril had always said, the person of Jesus was the person of the Son. The human eating, suffering, and dying of Jesus were the actions of one *divine person* in His human nature.[43] In clarifying these things, the council condemned both Nestorianism and Monophysitism in line with Chalcedon. The writings of Theodore of Mopsuestia were condemned and it was affirmed that 'one of the Trinity suffered in the flesh'.[44] The Council agreed: 'If anyone does not confess his belief that our

---

43. For more, see Fairbairn and Reeves, Creeds, 143–149; Wellum, *God the Son Incarnate*, 313–324.

44. This was the catchphrase of some Scythian monks. See J. A. McGuckin, 'The "Theopaschite Confession" (Text and Historical Context): a Study in the Cyrilline Re-interpretation of Chalcedon', *Journal of Ecclesiastical History* 35, no. 2 (1984): 239–255.

Lord Jesus Christ, who was crucified in his human flesh, is truly God and the Lord of glory and one of the members of the holy Trinity: let him be anathema.'[45]

The Third Council of Constantinople (680–681) affirmed that, because of His two *natures*, Christ had two *wills*: one human and one divine. Some had suggested that Christ had only one 'energy' or 'activity', and any human will was subsumed into the preceding divine will. This came to be called 'Monothelitism' (*mono* = one; *thelema* = will) and was briefly held as imperially sanctioned doctrine.[46] Maximus the Confessor (c.580–662) argued against it, tracking with the soteriological objection to earlier Apollinarianism: if Christ did not assume a human will, then the human will is 'unhealed' or cannot be saved. But he also sketched out a significant theological argument. The Trinity, he said, is three persons sharing one divine nature and one will, otherwise there would be three individual wills in the Trinity, all potentially at loggerheads, risking a kind of tritheism. This follows that a *will* must belong to a *nature* rather than a *person*. In other words, Christ must have both His divine will as the Son, as well as a newly assumed *human* will to be the Saviour of the whole human person. To speak in this way is not to court Nestorianism, since His two wills are not the functions of two *persons* in the Son, but of His two *natures*.[47] While Maximus' theology was rejected by the Byzantine authorities during his life, at the Third Council of Constantinople, he was judged to have been right, and entirely in line with Leo's *Tome*, Cyril's letters, and the Council of Chalcedon. Maximus' thinking helps us to be clear when we speak about Christ in His two natures. It

---

45. Canon X of the Second Council of Constantinople (381) quoted in Norman P. Tanner (ed.), *Decrees of the Ecumenical Councils Volume 1: Nicaea I to Lateran V* (Washington: Georgetown University Press, 1990).

46. See Wellum, *God the Son Incarnate*, 340–342.

47. See Wellum, *God the Son Incarnate*, 342–348; Demetrios Bathrellos, *The Byzantine Christ: Person, Nature, and Will in the Christology of Saint Maximus the Confessor* (Oxford: Oxford University Press, 2004).

would not be right to say that 'The humanity of Christ died on the cross' since natures don't act, only *persons* do. It was *Christ* who died, in a human way and according to His human nature. Equally it would not be right to say that, in Gethsemane, the Father and Son parted company as they appear to will different things (Luke 22:42). Rather, as the Son prayed 'Not my will, but yours, be done', the Lord was sanctifying His human will to the Father and learning obedience with it in this most demanding moment of pain and temptation.[48]

Questions about Christology, persons, natures, the communication of idioms, and more all continued through the centuries. They hung over the prayerful theology of Anselm as he pondered why and how God became man. They echo through the halls of the *Summa* of Thomas Aquinas. They animated the in-house disagreements between the reformers of the sixteenth century as Luther, Zwingli, and Calvin came to different conclusions about the Lord's Supper.[49] While languages and ideas change according to context, one thing is noteworthy. In every argument and in every era, every theologian hopes to prove that Cyril of Alexandria is in his corner.

---

48. See D. Glen Butner Jr., *The Son Who Learned Obedience: A Theological Case Against the Eternal Submission of the Son* (Eugene: Pickwick Publications, 2018), 72–76.

49. For an argument that Cyril taught something close to the *extra Calvinisticum*, see Andrew McGinnis, *The Son of God Beyond the Flesh: A Historical and Theological Study of the Extra Calvinisticum* (London: Bloomsbury, 2014), 15–46.

AFTERWORD

Today, Cyril's theology is as rich a resource as ever. There are plenty of ways he can be a help and encouragement to the Church in our day.

Cyril's thought can act as a litmus test for our preaching, teaching, praying, and writing. When popular teachers claim that Jesus 'laid his divinity aside as He sought to fulfil the assignment given to Him by the Father' and that the anointing of the Holy Spirit 'was what linked Jesus, the man, to the divine,'[1] we can turn to Cyril for scriptural clarity and correction.[2] When a theologian we admire and respect, like the puritan John Owen, writes that 'the only singular immediate act of the person of the Son on the human nature was the assumption of it into subsistence with himself,' and that, on the cross, 'the human nature complained of its dereliction by the divine,'[3] Cyril's theology can help us navigate potential pitfalls. As we consider the doctrine of the eternal generation of the Son, debates about submission and authority in the Trinity, and questions about relationship of

---

1. Bill Johnson, *When Heaven Invades Earth: A Practical Guide to a Life of Miracles* (Shippensburg: Destiny Image Publishers, 2003), 79.

2. See also Jonathan Black, *Charismatics and the Ninth Anathema*, https://www. apostolictheology.org/2014/07/charismatics-and-ninth-anathema.html. Last accessed May 13, 2024.

3. John Owen, *Works of John Owen* vol. 3 (Edinburgh: Banner of Truth, 1965), 160–161. See also Oliver D. Crisp (ed.), *Revisioning Christology: Theology in the Reformed Tradition* (London: Routledge, 2021), 91–110; Reeves, *Introducing Major Theologians.*

philosophy to theology, Cyril's theological writings are a vital port of call. Beyond this, his biblical commentaries – so often underappreciated – beg to be mined for riches of exegesis and application.

More than that, though, Cyril's theology is a call to a broader, longer, higher, and deeper vision of Jesus Christ and a more wholehearted enjoyment of the love of God in Him.

One of the latest of Cyril's writings we have is his Festal Letter 30, most likely written in 442 (though usually erroneously listed as being from 444, the year of his death). In the letter, he expounds passages from the book of Hebrews, considers Christ's fulfilment of the Law, and the centrality of baptism. He writes that

> those who pronounce the profession of faith unwaveringly must, I claim, avoid being shaken from it in any way. For it is written, "My beloved brothers and sisters, be steadfast, immovable, always abounding in the work of the Lord."[4]

Perhaps Cyril was looking back and reflecting on his own ministry of steadfast defence of the faith as he goes on. 'There are some', he says, 'who divide him who is indivisible, the one Christ, and who pervert the splendid beauty of the truth'.[5] This beautiful truth is that while Christ 'appeared as a human being from a woman, as far at least as his body and appearance went', he

> had a glory completely befitting the divine, made splendid with the highest honors, fulfilling the Father's works. For the power to bring the dead to life when they are already foul with the stench of putrefaction, to send light into those deprived of eyesight, to render the lame sound of foot, and to free lepers of their disease with a touch and a word of command, dwells solely in that substance which is above all others.[6]

---

4.   Cyril, *Festal Letters* 13–30, 201 (quoting 1 Cor 15:58).

5.   Cyril, *Festal Letters* 13–30, 202.

6.   Cyril, *Festal Letters* 13–30, 203.

This glorious one,

> the very Word who is from God the Father, having become a human being on our account and for us, while remaining what he was, God that is, gave his own body to death, that he might ransom us from death and decay by his own blood... He was not, then, unaware that he would suffer. Able as he was to avoid the snares, therefore, he gave his own body willingly to death for a short time, so that, once raised from the dead, he might destroy the power of death, that he might undo the devil's envy, through which death entered human nature, and that he might refashion us unto incorruptibility and everlasting life.[7]

It is as good a summary as any of the theology he unwaveringly held to throughout his life. The one Lord Jesus Christ is the glory of His Father and the redeemer of humanity. Cyril's view of Jesus is big enough for Him to be the perfect revelation of God – even (and especially!) in His humanness, suffering, and death. It is big enough to for him to bring divine and human together in the meeting place of the incarnation. But more than having just a high and holy view of Christ and a 'big' God, Cyril's vision was of a good God. A God who was good enough not only to give but *personally* secure our union, adoption, intimacy, and eternal happiness in His own presence. He did not do all this at a distance from us or wearing gloves to handle us, but by the life, death, and resurrection of the man from Nazareth: God with us.

God did not *need* to behave in this way towards us. He would surely have been happy and satisfied in the eternal, glorious fellowship of the Trinity. Yet, it is God's desire that, in Jesus and by the Spirit, His eternal glory and life overflow to us. It is nothing short of amazing grace and the most tender compassion.

---

7. Cyril, *Festal Letters* 13–30, 202, 205.

Christian Focus Publications

Our mission statement –

STAYING FAITHFUL

In dependence upon God we seek to impact the world through literature faithful to His infallible Word, the Bible. Our aim is to ensure that the Lord Jesus Christ is presented as the only hope to obtain forgiveness of sin, live a useful life and look forward to heaven with Him.

Our Books are published in four imprints:

CHRISTIAN FOCUS

popular works including biographies, commentaries, basic doctrine and Christian living.

CHRISTIAN HERITAGE

books representing some of the best material from the rich heritage of the church.

MENTOR

books written at a level suitable for Bible College and seminary students, pastors, and other serious readers. The imprint includes commentaries, doctrinal studies, examination of current issues and church history.

CF4•K

children's books for quality Bible teaching and for all age groups: Sunday school curriculum, puzzle and activity books; personal and family devotional titles, biographies and inspirational stories – because you are never too young to know Jesus!

Christian Focus Publications Ltd,
Geanies House, Fearn, Ross-shire,
IV20 1TW, Scotland, United Kingdom.
www.christianfocus.com